Warrior Chiefs of Southern Africa

SHAKA OF THE ZULU · MOSHOESHOE OF THE BASOTHO ·
MZILIKAZI OF THE MATABELE · MAQOMA OF THE XHOSA

IAN J. KNIGHT

Firebird Books

First published in the United Kingdom in 1994 by Firebird Books
P.O. Box 327, Poole, Dorset BH15 2RG

Copyright © 1994 Firebird Books Ltd
Text copyright © 1994 Ian J. Knight

Distributed in the United States by
Sterling Publishing Co. Inc.
387 Park Avenue South, New York, NY 10016-8810

Distributed in Australia by
Capricorn Link (Australia) Pty Ltd
P.O. Box 6651, Baulkham Hills, NSW 2153

British Library Cataloguing in Publication Data
Knight, Ian, 1956–
    The warrior chiefs of Southern Africa.
    I. Title
    355.009684

ISBN 1-85314-106-2

Designed by Kathryn S.A. Booth
Typeset by Dorwyn Ltd, Rowlands Castle, Hants
Monochrome origination by Castle Graphics, Frome
Printed and bound in Great Britain by The Bath Press

Contents

Shaka of the Zulu 7

Moshoeshoe of the BaSotho 51

The bay of Port Natal, as it looked twenty years after the first English expedition under George Farewell in 1824. European impact on the peoples of Southern Africa was still minimal and this idyllic lagoon was the only variable port along the Natal and Zululand coast. It is now the city of Durban.

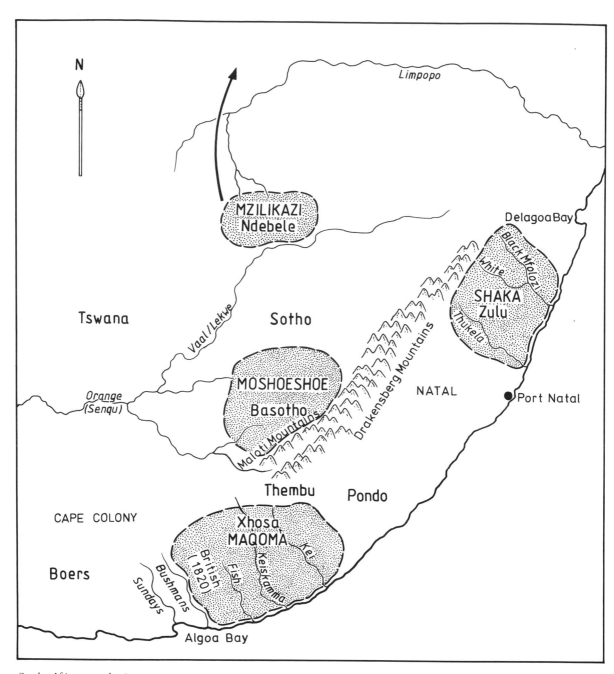

South Africa around 1830, showing the locations of various peoples of the period.

Shaka
OF THE ZULU

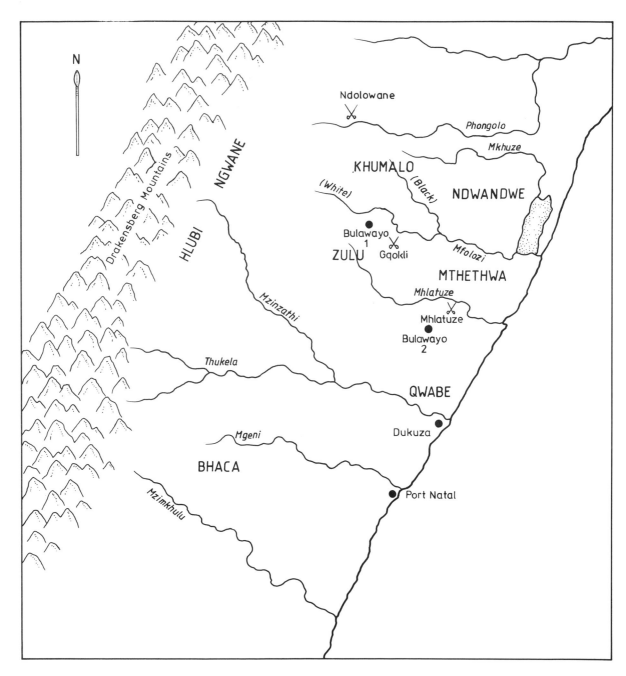

*Territories of the major clans
in Zululand during the reign
of King Shaka.*

He was powerfully built and had a bad temper. His strength was remarkable . . . Shaka was an expert performer, able to dance and sing . . .

(Madikane ka Mlomowetole)

[Shaka was] a savage in the truest sense of the word . . . without one virtue to redeem his name
(Nathanial Isaacs)

The Heavens that Thundered

King Shaka kaSenzangakhona of the Zulu is arguably the most famous black leader of nineteenth-century South Africa. His achievements were astonishing. When he came to the throne in 1816, the Zulus were a small clan largely unknown beyond their immediate neighbours. When he was assassinated twelve years later, his power extended over hundreds of square miles, and his armies were feared from Portuguese Delagoa in the north to the Cape frontier in the south. The political and military system he created survived him by sixty years, despite a rapidly changing world which brought it into conflict with encroaching Boers and Britons. It was finally destroyed in 1879 only when confronted by the world's most sophisticated military technology. In South Africa today, King Shaka remains an enormously potent political image, an archetypal warrior, a symbol of black power and independence, and his life has been the subject of biographies, poems, novels, plays and films. So wrapped round has he become with mythology and legend, in fact, that it is difficult to peel away the layers of folklore to reveal the truth about this extraordinary man. This is a task that has been made all the more difficult by a deliberate and sustained attempt to distort the historical record and besmirch the king's reputation, to present him as the cruel and inhuman product of a worthless and degraded culture. This distortion is particularly difficult to eradicate because it goes right back to our earliest descriptions of Shaka. We have only three contemporary written accounts of his reign, by British travellers who made the dangerous journey to his court at the height of his power. One, Nathanial Isaacs, set the tone for most future portraits when he wrote in his *Travels and Adventure in Eastern Africa*:

[Shaka was] a savage in the truest sense of the word, a monster, a compound of vice and ferocity without one virtue to redeem his name from the infamy to which history will consign it.

This image of Shaka as bloodthirsty barbarian has coloured our understanding of him across a century and a half. Yet Isaacs was scarcely a credible witness. He was only seventeen when he first arrived in Zululand, an unabashed adventurer, who once urged his fellow diarist, Henry Francis Fynn, to

Make them [The Zulu Kings] out to be as blood-thirsty as you can and endeavour to give an estimate of the number of people they killed during their reign, and also describe the frivolous crimes people lose their lives for. It all tends to swell up the work and make it interesting.

Fortunately, Fynn does not seem to have taken his advice entirely, and his famous *Diary* remains a more reliable source, though scarcely without flaws. The original manuscript was lost – buried by mistake, wrapped in an elephant's ear, in the grave of his brother, according to one romantic story – and the published version was compiled years later from fragmentary notes and memory. By then, the passing of the time seems to have exaggerated in his mind many of the extraordinary events Fynn witnessed. The third (recently rediscovered) account is that of 'John Ross'.

To find a true picture of Shaka, one must look beyond these blinkered and incomplete portraits, and try to locate him in his own culture and time. This is not easy, and many of the facts will never now be known for sure, but we are fortunate to have a good deal of evidence from Zulu sources, recorded at the turn of the century. Some of these Zulus remembered Shaka from their childhood; others had been given detailed accounts of his reign by their fathers, some of whom held high positions in his court. In a culture accustomed to recording history orally, their descriptions afford us a rare insight into Shaka's kingdom.

From these accounts Shaka emerges as a man of tremendous physical and mental strength, with an undeniably daunting personality:

He was powerfully built and had a bad temper. His strength was remarkable, for he could, when examining a beast, lift up its leg by one arm and look under it. Only Ngomane kaMqoboli ever dared answer him back among the Zulu. Even his own relations were afraid to do so.

Scarred by his childhood experiences of rejection and fiercely ambitious, he was certainly a ruthless and dangerous man. That he not only survived the turmoil of the first, main phase of Zulu expansion but emerged a winner testifies to his dynamic military skills. He was not afraid to wage war to the death, and instinctively understood the value of terror as a political tool in the art of empire building. His capacity for capricious violence is the most frequently discussed aspect of his reign, and, while many tales of his massacres are absurdly sensational, there is no doubt he never tolerated any slight to his dignity:

Shaka was an expert performer, able to dance and sing. Shaka composed a song about Lubedu [a Chief who had come to pay him tribute] which was to be danced the next day . . . Lubedu laughed. Shaka said 'So, the small fat toad is laughing at me!' (for Lubedu was short). 'Take him away', said Shaka, whereupon he was killed, for laughing at the King, and yet he was only laughing because he approved of what the king did.

Madikane kaMlomowetole

But such behaviour must be set against the background of his personal

history, and in the context of his turbulent times. Suggestions that he was incapable of forming ordinary human relationships are discounted by a wealth of evidence to the contrary. Throughout his life he remained close to the female relatives, particularly his mother and grandmother, who had shared the hardships of his youth, and he persistently refused to act against his half-brothers, though they were an obvious focus for political discontent. The occasional misdemeanors of his favourite warriors were greeted with tolerant good humour, and when the whites first arrived in his territory he treated them with a courtesy and generosity their actions did not always warrant. There are many folk tales, too, which speak of his wisdom, humour and benevolence, enough to suggest that he was not without such qualities – nor could he have been, to have attained his position and stayed there so long.

Finally, what sort of man was he physically? A Zulu named Baleka kaMpitikazi, whose father had served Shaka in the Fasimba regiment, and knew him well, has left us a rather unflattering portrait, which is nonetheless consistent with other sources:

My father used to say that Shaka was a tall man, dark, with a large nose, and was ugly. He spoke with an impediment (i.e. mouthed his words, as if his tongue was too big for his mouth, and pressed on his teeth).

By all accounts, King Shaka was a remarkable man, and one whom history has not always treated fairly.

Henry Francis Fynn, one of the British adventurers who first came to Shaka's court in 1824. Many of them adopted African lifestyles, and, as their clothes wore out, their appearance became increasingly bizarre. Fynn is described as having habitually worn nothing more than a blanket and a crownless straw hat.

Zululand

The area now known as Zululand lies on the southeastern coast of Africa, between the Drakensberg mountains and the Indian Ocean. It is steep, rolling downland, which drops in a series of terraces, from cool inland heights to a subtropical coastal belt. It is well watered, and a series of major river systems have cut deep, often spectacular gorges on their way to the sea. Before agricultural activity drastically altered the region's botanical make-up, the hot river valleys were covered in thorn-bush, and dense forests crested the intersecting ridges. Wildlife was abundant, but, most significantly, Zululand possessed a rich range of grasses which matured throughout the year, making it ideal cattle country.

The role of cattle in the African societies of southern Africa cannot be overemphasized. Among the Nguni, the cultural and linguistic group to which the Zulus belong, they not only provided food – the staple diet, milk curds *amaSi*, and meat – and hides for cloaks, sandals and shields, but they were also a means of assessing social worth. Since an exchange of cattle was a crucial part of the marriage ceremony, the abundance of cattle dictated in very real terms the speed at which the human population expanded.

It is difficult to say with certainty when the Nguni first settled in Zululand. Bronze-age deposits have been found dating to the sixth century, and by the fifteenth century the accounts of shipwrecked sailors – the only contacts between this part of Africa and the outside world – describe African inhabitants whose life-style was clearly Nguni. They lived in family homesteads (*umuzi*, plural *imizi*), each

one a collection of neatly thatched domed huts, arranged in a circle around a central cattle pen, and surrounded by a stout stockade for protection. The family head lived at the top end, opposite the entrance, with perhaps two or three wives, and his offspring and attendants on either side, in order of seniority. Families who claimed descent from a common ancestor constituted a clan, and each clan was ruled by a hereditary chief.

When each son in a homestead married, so he set out to build his own umuzi, in a process of constant expansion. Thus, according to tradition, a man named Malandela, who lived on the upper Mhlatuze River sometime in the seventeenth century, fathered two sons. Qwabe and Zulu. Both in due course founded homesteads of their own, which in time became the focus of clans that still bear their names; Zulu, whose name means *the Heavens*, settled on the south bank of the White Mfolozi, and his people took the name *abakwaZulu*, 'they of Zulu's place', or, more simply, *amaZulu*, 'Zulu's people'.

As the cattle thrived in fertile Zululand, so the people grew. Yet there were ecological limits. Much of the grass cover was surprisingly fragile, and intensive grazing made the soil vulnerable to the heavy downpours of the wet season, which stripped the hills to their skeletal boulders, and scarred the landscape with *dongas*, deep run-off gulleys. Pasture failed to regenerate. The process was made worse late in the eighteenth century by a series of droughts known as *Madlathule*, 'let him eat what he can, and say nought.' The combined effect of over-crowding and drought seems to have led to an increase in tension between Nguni clans, which paved the way for the rise of the Zulu. With too many cattle chasing too little pasture, clans were brought

Life in a Zulu village during the 1840s, sketched by the traveller George French Angas. The dome-shaped huts and reed screens are typical of nineteenth-century dwellings.

into open competition, and early in the nineteenth century this competition erupted into violence.

Two clans, in particular, emerge from this early period as prototype empire builders, who sought to maximize the land at their disposal by extending control over their neighbours – the Mthethwa of Chief Dingiswayo, and the Ndwandwe of Chief Zwide. Dingiswayo is remembered as an astute politician, whose success was based on a series of shrewd alliances, backed by force where necessary. His opponent, Chief Zwide, on the other hand, has come down to us as a rather less savoury character, whose success owed much to the fearsome reputation his mother enjoyed as a sorceress. Queen Nthombazi is said to have kept the skulls of Zwide's more important vanquished enemies in her hut, in order to transfer their psychic power to her son. Some historians have also suggested that Zwide was further motivated by involvement in the clandestine slave trade, which operated from Portuguese Delagoa.

The Zulus themselves were a small and insignificant clan whose territory lay west of the Mthethwa and south of the Ndwandwe. They accepted shelter under the Mthethwa umbrella, but took no part in this dangerous power play. Until the advent of Shaka.

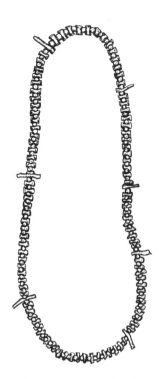

A necklace of small, interlocking wooden beads – one of the distinctions awarded to warriors for outstanding bravery in the days of the old Zulu kingdom.

Birth and Childhood

One day in the 1780s, Prince Senzangakhona kaJama, the heir to the chieftainship of the Zulu, was out herding cattle with the companions of his age-set. It had been their practice to drive the cattle to the same spot every day, and they had attracted the attentions of girls from the neighbouring Langeni clan, with whom they would flirt. The prince was young, perhaps still in his teens, handsome, not yet married, but probably looking for a wife, and he paired off with a girl named Nandi, *the Sweet One*. Nguni custom allowed limited lovemaking, *soma*, outside marriage, providing pregnancy did not ensue. Within a few months it became clear that the couple had allowed passion to get the better of them, however. Nandi tried to conceal her condition by claiming that she was merely suffering from an intestinal ailment, an *itshaka*, but in due course she gave birth to a baby boy, whom she ironically named Shaka. Nandi's family sent a message to the Zulu prince informing him of his responsibility. By that time, Senzangakhona had already married, but he duly accepted Nandi into his household.

By all accounts, however, Shaka had a miserable childhood. Deeply proud and well aware of his royal blood, he was nevertheless resented

by the Zulus, and grew up aloof, lonely and quarrelsome. He was still young when Nandi returned to the Langeni and took him with her. The circumstances surrounding her marriage seem to have soured her relationship with her husband, and, with the onset of the Madlathule, the Zulus had no spare food for the unwelcome. Among the Langeni, Shaka found comfort with his grandmother, but he was no more popular with boys of his own age, who bullied and victimized him. Once, at mealtime, they had forced him to hold out his cupped hands, into which they poured scalding hot curds. Even at this age, Shaka was not one to take such treatment lightly, and his fearsome temper eventually got the better of him, and led to his expulsion from the clan once more. Shaka had fought with another boy over a traditional game in which stones represent cattle, and circles scratched in the dirt, homesteads. The other boy stole Shaka's stones and, in a fury, Shaka snatched up a spear and stabbed a beast belonging to the boy's family. This was a terrible crime for a herdboy, especially in a time of want, and Shaka and Nandi found themselves outcasts again. These years of rejection, wandering in search of a protector, left a deep psychological scar on Shaka.

They found a refuge at last amongst the Mthethwa, in the homestead of Ngomane kaMqoboli, one of Chief Dingiswayo's principle advisers. Ngomane treated Nandi with respect, and he seems to have filled the role of a missing father figure in Shaka's life. Shaka grew up strong and

Ndwandwe commander, based on a description of Soshangane by a British Naval party who encountered him at Mozambique, fleeing from the Ndwandwe defeat by Shaka at the battle of Mhlatuze. He is wearing an ornate costume comprising a double kilt made of twisted animal tails. It differs only in detail from a description of Shaka's costume, suggesting the similarity of Zulu and Ndwandwe styles, even at this period.

15

Warriors skirmishing: until Shaka invented his revolutionary fighting techniques, battles in the nineteenth century consisted of an exchange of throwing spears; close combat was rare.

ambitious among the Mthethwa, and when the time came to *kleza*, to 'drink milk from the udders of the chief's cows', and offer service in return, he naturally reported to Dingiswayo rather than Senzangakhona.

Every few years, it was the custom for Nguni chiefs to summon all the youths who had reached the age of seventeen or eighteen and form them into a guild known as an *ibutho* (pl. *amabutho*). This was a form of national service, a means by which a chief could exercise some control over his clan manpower. Until such time as he gave them permission to marry, a chief could call on his amabutho to act as the labour gang of the clan. They kept the chief's homesteads in order, tended his crops, took part in hunts, policed his citizens, and fought his wars. It was this last aspect of his duties that appealed to Shaka. With the rise of the Mthethwa, armed conflict was on the increase, and the amabutho were being used more and more in their military capacity. Dingiswayo is thought to have been the first to use them as battlefield tactical units, effectively turning mere guilds into organized regiments.

Zulu man photographed late in the nineteenth century, carrying both a throwing spear and a stabbing spear.

The Young Warrior

Nguni warfare at the start of the nineteenth century had a strong ritualistic content. Rival armies would meet at an appointed place and time, accompanied by a crowd of civilian supporters. The exchange would begin with a prolonged harangue, in which champions would extol their own virtues, insult their enemies and issue personal challenges. The actual fighting consisted of hurling light throwing spears, which were easily parried on oval cowhide shields. Casualties were light, and moral ascendancy, not massacre, was the order of the day.

It is usually Shaka who is given the credit for changing all this:

Everyone was taught by Shaka what true bravery was. He made them throw away their many assegais and ordered that each man was to carry only one assegai.

Mayinga kaMbekuzana

Perhaps, as the struggle for natural resources turned increasingly into a struggle for survival, the rather gentlemanly conventions of old were already passing away. Nonetheless, there can be no doubt that Shaka liked fighting. He seems to have found an outlet for his frustrations in the physical contact of battle, and he preferred to charge down on his enemy and fight at close quarters. At that time, warriors still wore hide sandals, which impaired their movement, and Shaka considered the light throwing spears, which often broke under the heavy thrusts of hand-to-hand combat, to be absurd toys. His solution was typically radical – he invented a whole new system of fighting.

It was based on a new weapon, specifically designed for stabbing. Shaka's celebrated stabbing spear was destined to have an astonishing impact on the history of the Nguni. Such spears were not unknown, but whether he alone conceived the idea is immaterial – he was certainly the first to have fully thought out its potential. Many African societies regard the forging of metal with superstitious awe, and it is scarcely surprising that the creation of Shaka's blade is surrounded by dark tales of magic and witchcraft. Shaka is said to have sought out a smith with a particularly grim reputation, who used human fat – the most potent war medicine – to temper the blade. The resulting weapon had a blade some eighteen inches long by an inch-and-a-half wide, mounted on a stout haft two-and-a-half feet long. Wielded overarm, the stabbing motion was awkward and weak, but thrust underarm, with the bodyweight behind it, it was extremely powerful. Shaka also increased the size of the shield, making it large enough to shelter the whole body behind. With practice, shield and spear could be used together in a brutally effective combat technique. Charging down on

Zulu blacksmith at work, photographed at the turn of the century. Iron ore was collected from surface deposits, and smelted in a clay furnace, into which air was pumped with goatskin bellows, as seen here. The smith's art was regarded with superstitious awe by the rest of the population.

Shaka's 'tactical edge', an impressive selection of stabbing spears. The blades were designed to be heavy and strong enough to withstand the brutal nature of Zulu hand-to-hand fighting.

his foe, Shaka could batter him with the shield, hooking the edge over that of his opponent and dragging it to the left. The enemy warrior would be thrown off balance, his own shield blocking his movements, and his left side exposed to Shaka's thrust.

When Shaka was confident he could handle his new weapon properly, he tried it out on the battlefield. He had not informed Dingiswayo of his plans, and the chief's reaction was a mixture of surprise and delight:

Dingiswayo sent out a force to attack Malusi of the Nxumalo people. Shaka went on this occasion, and that is where he began the battle. On this occasion he rushed forward alone into the enemy and started stabbing about. Dingiswayo reproved him, he said that being a Chief's son he should not go forward alone.

Another impi left Dingiswayo to attack Pakatwayo, and fought an engagement at the Mhlatuze. Shaka again went forward and attacked. Pakatwayo was defeated. Dingiswayo found out that Pakatwayo's impi ran off because of Shaka . . . Dingiswayo now named Shaka by saying 'Shaka who is not beaten, the axe that surpasses other axes, the impetuous one who disregards warnings.'

Mayinga kaMbekuzana

Thus Shaka's reputation spread throughout the Mthethwa confederacy. He was known as *Sikithi*, 'the Finisher-Off', or 'the Hoe that Surpasses Other Hoes' – an illusion to the way he stabbed freely about him in battle – and 'the Heavens [i.e. Zulu] that Thunder in the Open'. He became a favourite of Dingiswayo, who raised him to the command of an ibutho, and shrewdly foresaw his wider potential. As the Mthethwa expanded, so it became necessary to extend a greater control over the Zulu. Dingiswayo invited Senzangakhona to a wedding dance, and carefully stage-managed a reunion between Shaka and his father. The young warrior danced a solitary war dance, *giya*, before Senzangakhona, and then boldly demanded a spear from him. That night, legend has it, Shaka secretly climbed onto the roof of the hut where his father was staying, to gain supernatural ascendancy over him. The significance of this was not lost on Senzangakhona, who realized that Dingiswayo was publicly indicating his candidature for the Zulu succession. Curiously enough, Senzangakhona, who cannot have been a very old man, died shortly after. He nominated a legitimate son, Sigujana, to succeed him, but Sigujana was mysteriously killed one day, and sometime in 1816 Shaka marched into his father's homestead at the head of a Mthethwa impi, to claim his inheritance.

The Zulu attack formation – the impondo zankomo *'beast's horns'. A strong body, usually composed of senior warriors, made a frontal assault on the enemy, whilst the 'horns', composed of young warriors, rushed out on either side.*

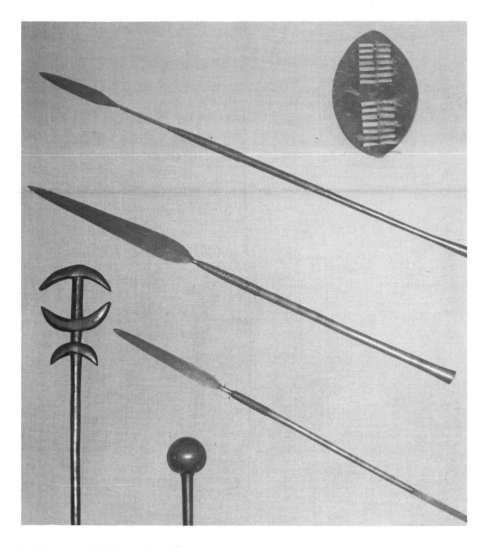

Rise of the Zulu

Shaka was still, of course, a vassal of Dingiswayo, but his ambition was not satisfied by control of the small clan his father ruled. He immediately summoned the clan's amabutho, and found perhaps four hundred warriors at his disposal. He carefully explained to them his new fighting system, and, while the stabbing spears were being manufactured, he instituted a rigorous training programme. The warriors were made to discard their sandals, and, to harden their feet, they were ordered to stamp flat thorns strewn across Shaka's cattle kraal. When they had learned to run barefoot, Shaka led them on long route marches across country. Finally, they were trained in a new attack formation, the *impondo zankomo*, or 'beasts' horns'. One body, known as the 'chest' and composed of senior warriors, would rush

A selection of Zulu weapons, including a throwing spear, two stabbing spears, and a knobkerry. The object on the left is a chief's staff.

19

straight at the enemy, while on either side two flanking parties, composed of younger warriors and called the 'horns', would rush out and surround the enemy. A fourth body, the 'loins', was kept in reserve. From the very beginning, Shaka enforced the strictest discipline, and disobedience and cowardice were punishable by death. If this methods were harsh, they were effective:

People could not run formerly, Shaka taught them to run; also his warriors were taught to run. He taught his men to do as he used to do when among the Mthethwas. He taught the attack to take place by running sharply. They used to run sharply to the attack with shields tucked under the arm . . . they would bring them out when they got among the enemy. In the attack they would run in a stooping position and at a great rate.

Mayinga kaMbekuzana

The first to feel Shaka's wrath were his mother's people, the Langeni. They were surrounded and overwhelmed before they could put up any serious resistance. Many stories are told about the revenge Shaka wreaked on his childhood persecutors; most of them are probably exaggerated, but he undoubtedly took the opportunity to settle old scores. He then turned his attention to his neighbours, and in quick succession defeated the Qwabe and Buthelezi clans.

A very unusual photograph of an impi, taken in the 1860s. It is not clear if these men are warriors in the Zulu king's army, or retainers of a powerful Natal chief; but all are carrying full-sized war-shields and wearing regimental regalia. This is an almost unique image, a rare impression of how a Zulu army might have looked early in the nineteenth century.

In the meantime, the broader conflict between Dingiswayo and Zwide had been coming to a head. The Ndwandwe had been no less active than the Mthethwa in extending their control, and both sides had made exploratory moves against each other's vassals. About 1817, Dingiswayo resolved to attack Zwide, and, summoning his allies, he advanced into Ndwandwe territory. Shaka was apparently late reaching the rendezvous, however, and the Mthethwa army paused on the Ndwandwe borders. Here, for some unaccountable reason, Dingiswayo wandered off, accompanied only by his handmaidens. He blundered

into a patrol of the Ndwandwe amaPhela regiment, who captured him and took him to Zwide. Zwide was jubilant, and had no doubt that this coup was due to the magical influence of Queen Nthombazi, who had used the full range of her skills to deliver her son's enemy into his hands. Curious as these tales of witchcraft seem to modern ears, the Nguni believed in them implicitly, and even Dingiswayo resigned himself to his fate:

Then Zwide asked, 'Who is as great as you, Dingiswayo?' Dingiswayo replied, 'No, I am no longer as great as you, for I have left my people and my soldiers'. Zwide said, 'So, then, could I now fight with you, Dingiswayo?' The latter answered, 'No, I no longer say that I can fight with you'.

Makuza kaMkomoyi

Zwide entertained his prisoner well for a few days, while he sought the advice of his councillors. Then he had him killed, and his skull was added to Queen Nthombazi's collection.

When news of Dingiswayo's death reached Shaka, he cried out 'Zwide has killed my father!'. No doubt he was genuinely shocked, but he could hardly have been unaware of the political implications. The whole of the Mthethwa confederacy was up for grabs. What's more, with the Mthethwa demoralized and confused, only Shaka's army stood between Zwide and mastery of the heart of Zululand. Zwide saw this too and in April 1818 he sent an army against Shaka. Shaka met it on a rocky eminence south of the White Mfolozi, known as Gqokli Hill.

The summit of Gqokli Hill, where Shaka's army first proved itself against the Ndwandwe in 1818. The Zulus are said to have formed a defensive circle on the upper slopes, with a strong reserve in a central depression, which cannot be seen from below.

21

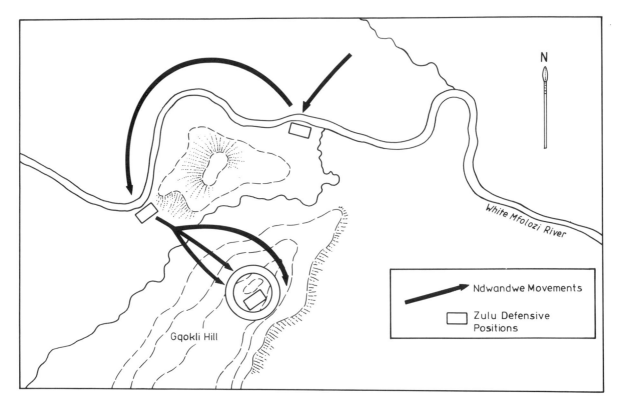

The map shows the battle of Gqokli Hill, with labels "N", "White Mfolozi River", "Gqokli Hill", and a legend showing "Ndwandwe Movements" and "Zulu Defensive Positions".

Struggle with the Ndwandwe

The battle of Gqokli Hill, Shaka's first major victory over the Ndwandwe. There are no contemporary written accounts of the action; therefore, indicted troop movements are conjectures.

The battle of Gqokli Hill is one of three crucial battles that established Shaka's mastery over the Ndwandwe. Unfortunately, because it took place so early in his career, we know very few hard facts about it, though fictionalized accounts have become part of the Shaka epic. The hill itself is a small knoll cresting a ridge running down to the White Mfolozi. There is a rocky outcrop to one side of the summit, and the depressed shoulder between them cannot be seen from the lower slopes. According to the traditional account, Shaka deployed advanced parties to guard the river drifts, then drew up in a defensive position around the summit, with a reserve out of sight in the depression. His army had already grown from its initial size, and he had perhaps four thousand men at his disposal. The Ndwandwe army, commanded by Zwide's heir Nomahlanjana, and drawn from all his subject clans, was at least twice that size, and probably more.

The battle began with a Ndwandwe attack on the river drifts. The Zulu parties were easily overwhelmed, but they served to delay and disrupt the Ndwandwe advance. Nomahlanjana then weakened his force still further by despatching several regiments to round up Zulu cattle. He formed the remainder up at the base of Gqokli Hill, and launched the first of a series of frontal assaults. It was here that the

22

advantages of the new Shakan fighting techniques became apparent. As the Ndwandwe advanced up the slope, their front contracted, and their lines buckled. They paused when in range to fling their spears, which the Zulus mostly caught on their shields. Instead of throwing them back, the Zulus rushed down and engaged them in a brief but brutal bout of hand-to-hand fighting. The Ndwandwe fell back in confusion. They tried again, several times, trying to probe for weaknesses in Shaka's line. Each attack met with the same result. At last, Nomahlanjana is said to have formed part of his force into a column, and tried to punch a hole through the Zulu defences. It was the moment Shaka had been waiting for – he unleashed his fresh reserves, who streamed out in the 'chest and horns' formation and surrounded the Ndwandwe column. According to Shaka's praises, no less than five of Zwide's sons fell on the bloody slopes of Gqokli, including Nomahlanjana. It was a crushing blow and the remainder of the Ndwandwe army began to drift away from the field.

Yet the battle had not by any means been decisive. The two sides had fought each other to a standstill, but the Ndwandwe had managed to extricate a large portion of their force, and Shaka lacked the strength to pursue them. Moreover, the damage they had inflicted on Zulu homesteads and herds had been very great. Politically, Zwide still remained a threat, and in the aftermath of the battle Shaka moved swiftly to

Shangane chief and his councillors, photographed in the 1890s. The Shangane were one of the splinter kingdoms which emerged from the remnants of the Ndwandwe, and this photograph suggests perhaps the appearance of Zwide's warriors during their epic struggle against Shaka.

consolidate his position. The Mthethwa had not yet recovered from the shock of Dingiswayo's death, and in an ironic reversal of the ploy that had brought him to power, Shaka overturned his patron's legitimate successor and placed his own candidate on the Mthethwa throne. A number of smaller clans, sensing a rising star, hitched their fortunes to that of the Zulu.

The showdown with Zwide occurred during the next fighting season. The Ndwandwe are thought to have used the year's grace to reorganize along Zulu lines, adopting the larger Zulu shields and stabbing spears. They were commanded by two of Zwide's ablest generals, Soshangane and Zwagendaba. Nevertheless, Shaka was still more than a match for them. All Nguni armies provisioned themselves by foraging, and the Ndwandwe expected to survive in enemy territory by looting Zulu grain stores and cattle. As they advanced, however, Shaka fell back before them, taking his herds and grain with him. There was some skirmishing, but he refused to engage in a heavy battle, drawing the Ndwandwe farther and farther from their own borders. As they began to suffer from hunger and exhaustion, so Shaka harassed them, especially at night:

Shaka's impi in the meantime remained in the forest looking at what was going on. When night came on, Shaka's impi again attacked [the Ndwandwe camp], making use as before of their password [i.e. to identify their own warriors in the dark]. They once more stabbed Zwide's people a good deal. They again retreated to the forest and back to Shaka.

Jantshi kaNongila

Shaka led the Ndwandwe on a wild chase around some of the most rugged landmarks of Zululand, and when at last they tired of it and began to retreat, he struck them as they struggled across the Mhlatuze River:

The Ndwandwe came down the Gcongco ridge, passed Empandhleni, and reached the Thukela at Ndondondwana. They then turned about, climbed the Madungela, and went towards Maqonga, below the Komo; they went along the Mvuzane towards the Mhlatuze, where they turned about and set up camp. The Zulu watched them. The next day the Zulu approached, coming from Shaka at Eshowe . . . at dawn the next day the two armies met at Nomveve . . . [Shaka's warriors] fought fiercely with the enemy . . . The enemy retreated, then broke and fled. The Ndwandwe were utterly defeated. Ndwandwe and Zulu corpses were lying across one another where the armies had met.

Mangati kaGodide

Ndwandwe warrior as sketched in the 1820s by a member of a British Naval party, which encountered Soshangane's band of survivors from the battle of Mhlatuze. This is one of the earliest known depictions of an mfecane warrior. The difference in appearance between the Zulu and Ndwandwe warriors appears to have been minimal.

The victory was indeed a decisive one, and the Ndwandwe disintegrated. Soshangane and Zwagendaba gathered a nucleus of warriors around them and fled into Mozambique, where they would later carve out their own empires. Shaka moved quickly to attack the Ndwandwe heartland, but Zwide and some of his followers managed to slip away, and took refuge in the distant eastern Transvaal. There are many stories of the massacres Shaka inflicted on the remaining Ndwandwe population, most of them untrue. No doubt he would have purged the clan

24

of those loyal to the old regime, but enough of it survived for him to elevate a junior member of the royal house to the chieftainship, and incorporate it into his own kingdom. It was an impressive victory, and Shaka celebrated in appropriate style. A huge ceremonial victory hunt was organized, and warriors slaughtered lion, elephant and buck across the length and breadth of the country. The army was paraded in review, and the heroes and cowards were picked out. For the heroes there was reward in the form of cattle and distinctive insignia, but for the cowards there was a grim retribution:

> On coming back from this campaign . . . he said that the cowards should be picked out. The cowards were then separated. After this their left arms were held up, and they were stabbed under the armpits like goats, Shaka saying 'Let them feel the assegai!' They were then stabbed. These men would then be killed as if they were cattle.'

> Baleni kaSilwana

The isihlahla samagwala, *a kei-apple bush, still standing, where Shaka used to pass judgement on his warriors after their return from a campaign. His great Bulawayo homestead was on the hill beyond.*

Hitherto, Shaka had lived on the White Mfolozi, at a modest homestead called Bulawayo – 'He Who was Killed', a reference to the indignities of his youth. Now he felt confident enough to build a new capital. He moved south, choosing a spot high on a ridge commanding a stunning view over the misty blue Mhlatuze valley. The new Bulawayo, also known as Gibixhegu ('Take Out the Old Man', a sly allusion to his victory over Zwide), was indeed a fitting symbol of his power and prestige. It contained nearly 1,500 huts, and the outer palisade was nearly two miles in circumference.

25

The Crushing

With the Ndwandwe threat removed, Shaka was free to consolidate his power by attacking his remaining neighbours. Between 1819 and 1824 his armies embarked on a series of raids, pushing as far north as the Phongolo River, and increasingly south across the Thukela into Natal. It was here that the devastation wrought by his attacks was most severe. Some of the more powerful clans, like the Thembu and Chunu, attempted to make a stand, but were overrun and driven out. Many lesser clans abandoned their fields, and fled to inaccessible strongholds. Unlike Zululand, where subdued clans were incorporated into the body of the kingdom, in Natal Shaka was content to plunder. His armies destroyed hundreds of homesteads, and carried off thousands of cattle. The early struggles between the Mthethwa and the Ndwandwe had created shock waves which rippled through the black population across the country, and now Shaka's rise exaggerated the process. The agrarian life-style of the Nguni could not easily withstand dislocation, and some clans, cut off from their crops, began to attack their neighbours in a desperate struggle for food. Already the Ngwane and Hlubi, living in the Drakensberg foothills, had crossed the passes and fallen on the Sotho of the interior, and now the Natal clans shuffled south, crowding in on the amaMpondo kingdom 200 miles away. A few destitute refugees sought sanctuary among the Xhosa on the eastern Cape frontier.

By the time the main phase of Zulu expansion ended, in about 1824, some parts of Natal were completely depopulated apart from wretched bands of pathetic survivors, some of whom were reduced to cannibalism.

Small wonder that this period of terrible marauding is still known as *mfecane*, 'the crushing'.

King Shaka's personal staff. When King Cetshwayo was captured by British patrols at the end of the war of 1879, he was carrying this staff, which he explained had belonged to his uncle, Shaka.

Shaka's Kingdom

Shaka's kingdom went far beyond anything envisaged by Dingiswayo or Zwide. To outsiders, including the first white travellers to visit it, it seemed a rigid autocracy, where the king's word was law. In fact, the balance of powerful interests within the kingdom was more complex. It remained a conglomerate of small clans, and it is doubtful if Shaka ever managed to control them as completely as he would have wished. Those who had been defeated by Shaka had had their royal line interrupted, an old chief killed and replaced by a candidate acceptable to Shaka, but many had joined the kingdom as allies rather than subjects, and their chiefly line ruled unmolested. Clan chiefs retained considerable local power, though the amabutho system deprived them of the control of their young men of military age. They were represented on the *ibandla*, a council composed of *izikhulu*, or 'great ones', who advised the king. The tension between central and local authority was a feature of the Zulu state, and the king could ill afford to ignore the feelings of his ibandla, though the evidence suggests that Shaka intimidated his councillors with his fierce temper. One white observer noticed that an argument with his advisers led to several of them being executed – no doubt they were expendable men of junior rank, but the effect on the remainder can readily be imagined.

Overlaying this clan structure was the central administrative apparatus of the state, the means by which the king held his country together and controlled it. Scattered strategically about the country were the royal homesteads, the *amakhanda*. Physically, these were ordinary homesteads writ large, a collection of several hundred huts surrounding a large cattle pen and protected by a stockade. At the top end was the *isigodlo*, the king's personal quarters, where he or his household lived when in residence. Shaka usually gave control of individual ikhanda to his female relatives. The amakhanda served as barracks for the army, and as regional centres of royal authority.

This authority was transmitted through a class of state officials known as *izinduna* (sing. *induna*). These men were chosen by the king, and their position was not dependent on clan rank. Many were highborn, but Shaka frequently appointed commoners to important military or administrative positions if their talents warranted it. They owed their fortunes to the king himself, and they helped offset the influence of the regional chiefs.

At the centre of the system was the king himself. Tradition invested him with tremendous ceremonial power – he was the nation's mouthpiece in its dealings with the spirit world, and his role in the annual first-fruits ceremony, which ushered in the new harvest, was crucial. He was the ultimate legal court of appeal, the final decision in all matters of state rested with him, and he was the supreme commander of the army. Much of the character of each reign therefore depended on the personality of the king himself, and there is no doubt that Shaka ruled his country with an iron hand. Physically energetic and mentally alert, curious to all developments of political interest, and alive to the possibility of discontent, Shaka was often on the move, setting a pace which even his councillors found difficult to keep up with:

Shaka used to be very fond of going about visiting places. He sat very little indoors. He frequently went to sit by, and look at, the sea, and when it was sunset he used to start off home at a run, and his [personal attendants] were obliged to keep up the running, which was not stopped until [his homestead] was reached.

Makewu

The Zulus knew no judicial penalties except a fine in cattle, for minor

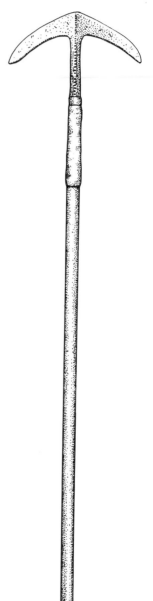

An iNhlenhla, a staff with a shaped iron head, carried as a mark of distinction by men of rank during the nineteenth century.

27

A famous incident from Shaka's reign, depicted in a dramatic nineteenth-century print: at a great 'smelling-out' ceremony called by the King, only one young sangoma *dares to identify Shaka himself as the man who defiled his own hut with blood.*

offences, or death for serious crimes. Shaka was not a cruel man or a sadist, as he has sometimes been portrayed, but he did use the death penalty freely. Executions were a daily occurrence at his court, part of a policy of maintaining power through terror. As one Zulu observed, 'he behaved thus as part of his government', though it is his more whimsical use of violence that is remembered today:

Shaka used to kill a man simply because he was ugly; not because he had practised witchcraft but merely because he had been born ugly. He would say, 'Hau! How ugly this fellow is! Take him away!' He would be killed even if he had done nothing. That man used to play around with people. A man would be killed though he had done nothing, though he had neither practised witchcraft, committed adultery, nor stolen.

Baleka kaMpitikazi

Harsh though they were, these methods seem to have been successful in suppressing political opposition and creating an ordered kingdom. White visitors were struck by the discipline and cleanliness of Shaka's subjects.

But if Shaka could be intimidating, he could also be solicitous of his subjects' welfare, no doubt with a view to maintaining their support. The majority of the population lived in dread of the *izangoma*, the diviners who 'smelt out' the activities of evildoers, and Shaka clearly resented their influence. One well-documented incident tells how he organized an elaborate hoax to expose the diviners as charlatans. One

28

night he smeared the entrance to his own hut with blood, a terrible superstitious omen, then organized a huge smelling-out ceremony, to identify the perpetrator. Diviner after diviner identified some innocent bystander, and only two young men guessed the truth. Shaka was generous in his rewards, indulgent of his favourites, and benevolent to those suffering genuine hardships. He held court every day during his morning bathe, or seated on a roll of matting, surrounded by attendants who held a shield over him, to shade him from the sun, and waited patiently to offer him snuff or beer. There were frequent cattle reviews, as carefully matched herds were brought from across the kingdom to be paraded in the capital, and the nights were alive with frequent dancing competitions. The king himself composed songs and orchestrated the dances, with hundreds of both sexes taking part. Woe betide anyone who spoiled his meticulous choreography – '[Shaka] would kill those who wilfully danced out of time with the others . . . on hearing him [Shaka] would get angry and put him to death.'

Perhaps the most conspicuous aspect of Shaka's state system, however, was the army. Initially, Shaka seems to have relied on amabutho drawn from allied clans to support his own purely Zulu forces, but, as his control over his subject chiefdoms became greater, so amabutho were recruited on the traditional age basis from all the clans in the kingdom. This had a number of political and military advantages.

Warrior from a young Zulu regiment in typical costume, wearing bunches of sakabuli *feathers in his headress, his body almost entirely covered by cow-tail ornaments. In later years, such regimental costumes were only worn on ceremonial occasions; but there is some evidence to suggest that part of it, at least, was worn into battle in Shaka's day.*

29

By monopolizing control of the most productive part of the community, the king greatly reduced the power of local chiefs, and transferred it instead to the state. Since each ibutho was composed of men from many different clans, it reduced the risk of disaffected clansmen drawing together within the army to subvert individual units. The warriors' common age encouraged a strong *esprit de corps*, and clan origins became subordinated to regimental loyalty. The amabutho remained in the king's service until he gave them permission to marry, at which point they dispersed and transferred their immediate allegiance to their families. Much nonsense has been written about the alleged celibacy of the Zulu warrior and its effect on his fighting spirit; in fact, Zulu moral codes allowed for limited sexual activity outside marriage and the amabutho system had less to do with sexual repression than with an attempt to resolve the conflict between state and family loyalty. By artificially prolonging bacherlorhood, Shaka maximized the time the warriors were under his direct command and also gained some control over the rate at which the nation reproduced itself. Shaka himself never married, nor did he father an heir, though he did wear the *isicoco* headring that signified a mature man. It is often suggested that he kept the entire male population under arms throughout his rule, yet this is clearly absurd. His reign was comparatively short, and the number of amabutho he was able to form was therefore limited; we also know that during his reign he allowed some of the older regiments to marry. The proportion of men in service at any given time was probably not much different to that during the reign of the later Zulu kings, although, unlike them, Shaka does seem to have required his active amabutho to be permanently mustered in the amakhanda. Married men constituted a reserve which might be mobilized in times of national emergency. When in the barracks, serving warriors were supposed to be fed at the king's expense, although many had to rely on supplies brought by members of their family. The huge herds looted in war were sorted according to the colour of their hides and distributed among the regiments, who were expected to look after them in return for using their milk products and occasional meat. The hides went to make warshields. The common age of the warriors, their successful record, and the terror this inspired outside the kingdom, all worked towards a high morale. Furthermore, the army ofered a potential for advancement not found elsewhere. Promotion, rewards of cattle, and even coveted insignia of bravery could all be earned by successful military service:

Ndengezi was a great warrior of Shaka's. He fought in the battle against Zwide. Shaka rewarded him with a number of cattle. Ndengezi was dissatisfied with the number that Shaka had given him because of the heroism he had displayed and the number he had killed. Shaka said 'But Ndengezi, are you the *only* warrior among all my people?' . . . Ndengezi's contention was that his reward should be such a number that a stick might be laid on their backs and carried off some distance . . . without falling to the ground. That was a worthy reward. . . .

Dinya kaZokozwayo

The relationship between the king and the amabutho was clearly mutually supportive. He looked to them as the basis of his power, and they looked to him for patronage and advancement. In Shaka's time, the Zulus became a very wealthy nation, a significant contrast to the days of the *Madlathule*.

Yet, however formidable Shaka's system was in its own world, fate was to introduce a new factor, even as his power was at its height. One day, it would seek to destroy all he had built up.

Coming of the Whites

Because Zululand was sealed off from the interior by the mountain barrier of the Drakensberg and cut off from the sea by the shoals and reefs of the 'wild coast', the momentous events of the 1810s and 1820s had gone largely unnoticed by the outside European world. The Portuguese explorer Vasco da Gama had first noted the existence of a distant line of green hills and crashing breakers when he rounded the Cape in 1497. Because he logged their discovery on Christmas Day, he called them Terra Natalis. The area south of the Thukela River is still known as Natal. Yet for three hundred years Europe took no interest in the region, and the only descriptions of it were from the survivors of occasional shipwrecks, who then made the perilous journey overland to the safety of the Cape or Portuguese Delagoa. Not until the first refugees from the mfecane fetched up at British frontier posts at the Cape did the authorities there show more than a flicker of curiosity. They remained primarily concerned with security on the frontier, but the tales of a fabulously powerful and wealthy African kingdom in the far north stirred the imagination of the merchant community.

Lieutenant Francis George Farewell, RN, who led a band of British and Afrikaner adventurers and traders to Shaka's kingdom in 1824.

The British empire was, at that time, awash with ex-servicemen looking to adventure to make their fortune. The Napoleonic Wars were not long over, and many a promising career had been cut short by premature retirement on half-pay. One such was Francis George Farewell, ex-Lieutenant, Royal Navy, who was so fascinated by stories of homesteads ringed with palisades of ivory that he organized an expedition to open commercial contacts with the Zulus. Natal had only one port, known to the Portuguese as Rio de Natal, and its practicability was so much in doubt that one recent survey had overlooked it completely. Yet when Farewell's advance party sailed across the sandy bar at its mouth in May 1824, they found its virtues to have been much underestimated. It was a beautiful, still lagoon, almost encircled by jaws of land, surrounded by exotic bush which teemed with game. Among the party was a diarist, Henry Francis Fynn. They spent the first night camped on the sand dunes, and their sleep was disturbed by hyenas,

31

Zulu knobkerries: (above) the iwisa was a simple club of polished wood with a knobbed end, used for fighting; (opposite) the larger example is believed to have been an executioners club.

who had to be driven off with flaming brands snatched from the fire. There were a few timid Africans living by the shore, who fled when Fynn mentioned Shaka's name. Undaunted, Fynn set off along the beach, accompanied by two servants, intending to walk to Shaka's homestead, which he imagined was only a few miles away. He had gone several miles when an extraordinary sight met his eyes:

I sat on the beach, and as I was looking across the sea, then at low tide, I saw on my right a dense mass of people coming fast from the direction I had taken. My view extended over several miles of the beach, but I could not see the rear of this immense black and continuous mass of natives, all armed and in their war-dresses. Our surprise was great and had I known the character of these people and the danger I was in, as I now know it, it is a question if I would have stood my ground, though an attempt to run away would not have saved me.

Fynn's companions fled into the bush and he was left to try and make himself understood by sign language. All he could work out was that the Zulu commanders recognized him as a potential source of beads, and that the name of Shaka had a magical effect. Then:

The leaders talked much among themselves, but at length passed on along the beach. This dense mass of natives continued to pass by me until sunset, all staring at me with amazement, none interfering with me.

Fynn later learned that this was an army returning from a raid against the amaMpondo in the far south. He followed them for a day or two, but was politely detained at the border while Shaka made preparations to meet him. During that time, the rest of Farewell's party arrived at the bay, and they were at last escorted together into Shaka's domain. The journey took several days, and it occurred to Fynn that they were being taken on a roundabout route, to impress them with the power and wealth of the kingdom. When they finally arrived at Bulawayo, the nation was gathered to greet them. It was an extraordinary spectacle, and they could not fail to be impressed:

The king came up to us and told us not to be afraid of his people, who were now coming up to us in small divisions, each driving cattle before it. The men were singing and dancing and whilst doing so advancing and receding even as one sees the surf do on a seashore. The whole country, as far as our sight could reach, was covered with numbers of people and droves of cattle. The cattle had been assorted according to their colour. . . .

It is difficult, now, to judge Shaka's attitude towards these whites, since we only have their side of the story on record. Certainly, Europeans were not unknown to the Zulus, who knew them as *abeLungu*, pallid and bedraggled sea-creatures, apparently washed up on the beach. It is unlikely that they made much impact on Shaka's day-to-day political affairs, preoccupied as these were with far more important matters. Yet there is no doubt that they arrived at a significant time – a period of stabilization after the rapid expansion – and that Shaka's policies looked increasingly towards the south. Certainly, the king was hungry for knowledge. Through an interpreter he questioned his guests closely on everything from European modes of government to the size of King George's house. He was certainly not overawed by their white skin, and listened to their answers with a good-humoured skepticism, concluding that they had little to equal the splendours of his own kingdom:

He desired to know from us if ever we had seen such order in any other state, assured us that he was the greatest king in existence, that his people were as numerous as the stars, and that his cattle were innumerable.

Most of all, he wanted to know about the European methods of making war, and demanded frequent demonstrations of firearms. On one occasion a lucky shot from a 'Brown Bess' musket fired by one of the party dropped an elephant in its tracks, and Shaka was suitably impressed. A Zulu source confirms this fascination, and perhaps suggests the real reason why Shaka adopted the whites:

Shaka liked Europeans, who were first reported to him as people white in colour, who had come out of the water and whose hair was like maize tassles. He was very much taken with the gun; he put up a shield, fired at it, examined the bullet mark on it then shot at a beast as a target and killed it. He called the white people *abakwetu* (i.e. people of our house).

Makwetu

However genuine his liking for the Europeans, Shaka undoubtedly considered them as providers of a useful addition to his military technology. Nor was he in the slightest bit fooled by their pretensions. Jokingly, he named one of the female guilds, the equivalent of the amabutho, *Nkisimana*, 'Englishmen'. More telling, however, was the name he gave to Nathanial Isaacs – *Dambuza Mthabathi*, 'He who Takes Things'.

And taking things was, of course, the main object of Farewell's party. If they had discovered that the tales of ivory palisades were untrue, they nevertheless found that elephant abounded in Natal, and that Shaka's country held all manner of other commercial attractions. In their campaign of acquisition, they were aided by a stroke of good fortune. Fynn had not long been at Bulawayo when, in the midst of a dance, Shaka was stabbed. The identity of the assailant has never been established, though the king had many enemies; Fynn blamed the Ndwandwe, while some Zulu traditions believe it was disaffected members of the Qwabe. The wound was not fatal, the spear passing through Shaka's arm and into his side, but the king sank into delirium and in Bulawayo pandemonium broke out. Fynn had some slight knowledge of medicine, and he bathed and bandaged the wound, and did his best to quiet the hysteria. Within a few days Shaka had recovered and order was restored, but it was in the aftermath of this attack that the whites presented Shaka with a petition begging for land. It was a long, rambling, pompous document which gave the whites possession of the bay, and a good stretch of the country round about. Shaka duly made his mark on the document, and Farewell ran up the Union Flag, and christened the bay Port Natal. This dubious transaction would later become the basis of all British territorial claims in the district.

It is unlikely that Shaka fully understood the significance of the document, nor, in all probability, would he have cared. The concept of individual land ownership was alien to Nguni culture. People came and went; the land remained. In so much as it was ownable at all, it was owned by the king in the name of the state, and he was at liberty to grant permision for specified districts to be settled and cultivated. That was a right which could be rescinded and the land given to someone else – as the Port Natal settlers would discover to their cost. Shaka merely recognized the services rendered by Farewell and Fynn and rewarded them with a *de facto* chieftainship in Natal. Having never experienced European military might, he had no reason to fear them, and so was unconcerned that they understood his actions differently. Indeed, the whites confirmed his view of them by adopting the lifestyle of local chiefs. They gathered supporters – refugees from Shaka's wars came out of the bush and joined them when it became clear they offered a safe haven – they amassed ivory and cattle, took African wives, and judged their subjects according to African law. In their memoirs, they were careful to present their activities in a favourable light, but they interfered in local politics, bullied their neighbours with the threat of Shaka's wrath, squabbled and bickered among themselves, and may even have tried to open Port Natal to the slave trade.

Shaka regarded them as no different to any other African group under his umbrella. His mistake would cost future generations of his people dear.

Last of the Ndwandwe

When Shaka defeated the Ndwandwe at Mhlatuze in 1819, Zwide himself had escaped to the Transvaal. Here he was able to regroup some of his followers and rebuild something of his old power. About 1825 Zwide died, and was succeeded by his son Sikhunyana. Sikhunyana was either an ambitious and vengeful young man, or life in the north was made intolerable by some unknown pressure, for he embarked on a campaign to regain control of the Ndwandwe ancestral lands. In 1826 news reached Bulawayo of their approach, and Shaka was furious: 'Shaka then said 'Oh! My [men]. I am going to war. I am making war on Sikhunyana. He has returned, for I drove out his father'. He then prepared the army and went off with it in the night.'

As he gathered his army, Shaka sent messengers to the whites at Port Natal, and ordered them to join him. They were horrified at the

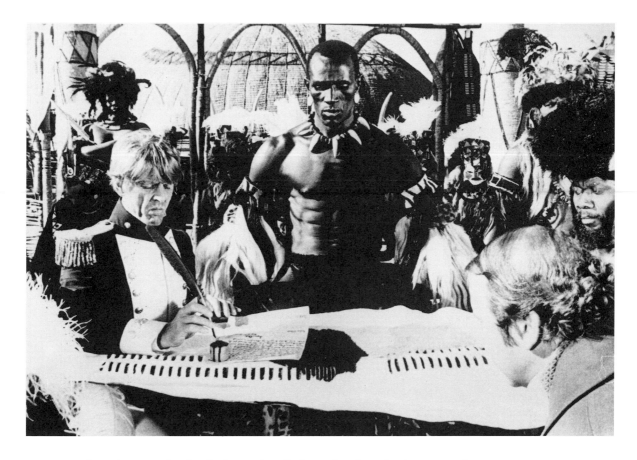

Shaka signs Farewell's document, giving Port Natal to the British; as reconstructed for the movie drama series Shaka Zulu. The series encapsulated the popular image of Shaka as both a heroic warrior and a despot.

prospect, but it was the logical result of the role they had accepted. They had achieved the status of chiefs as a gift from Shaka, partly because they had impressed him with their firepower. Now he expected them to serve him in return. Wriggle as they might, they could not escape their obligation, for Shaka could be most persuasive:

He showed us how dependent we were on him. He also pointed out that vessels seldom, or never, visited Natal; that he could destroy everyone of us in such a way that there would be no one left to tell the tale; and that, if the English should seek to avenge our being massacred, they would be terror-struck at the magnitude of his army. On Mr Farewell refusing to lend [the king's interpreter] a musket, one was taken from us by force. . . .

The whites had no choice but to comply. The army set off, accompanied by a huge crowd of camp followers, driving cattle and carrying food and baggage for the important warriors. Fynn estimated the total number of people involved as 50,000 – probably an over-estimate, although there is no doubt it was one of the largest Zulu forces yet fielded, reflecting Shaka's concern about the Ndwandwe threat. It was led by the king himself, and Fynn has left a vivid description of his magnificent war-dress:

Round his forehead was a turban [a padded headband] of otterskin, with a crane feather erect in

35

front, fully two feet long, and a wreath of scarlet feathers, formerly worn, only, by men of high rank. Ear ornaments made from dry sugar cane, carved round the edge, with white ends, and an inch in diameter, were let into the lobes of his ears, which had been cut to admit them. From shoulder to shoulder he wore bunches, five inches in length, of the skins of monkeys and genets, twisted like the tails of these animals. These hung half down the body. Round the ring on his head, were a dozen tastefully arranged bunches of loury feathers, neatly tied to thorns which were stuck in the hair. Round his arms were white tails, cut down the middle so as to allow the hair to hang about the arm, to the number of four for each arm. Round the waist there was a kilt or petticoat, made of skins of monkeys and genets, and twisted as before described, having small tassles round the top. The kilt reached to the knees, below which were white ox-tails fitted to the legs so as to hang down to the ankles. He had a white shield with a single black spot, and one assegai. When thus equipped he certainly presented a fine and most martial appearance.

The army advanced rapidly north, crossing the Ntombe River, and confronting the Ndwandwe at a hill named Ndolowane. This was to prove the last great battle Shaka controlled personally, but it showed no great tactical complexity. The Zulus formed up in their 'chest and horns' formation, and the battle was opened with a smattering of shots from the whites and their retainers. Then the Zulus charged. Fynn saw them fall back twice before a third attack burst through the Ndwandwe lines, and carried them in among the civilians. Certainly the carnage was bloody and comprehensive:

After being prepared, the troops left, forming two horns, and surounded that mountain. Before they could surround the mountain, Sikhunyana escaped. Shaka saw him flee. The two horns met, and began stabbing one another, for the people, being very numerous, did not know one another. But they soon discovered, and desisted. Sikhunyana himself had escaped but his impi had been hemmed in. 'Kill off every soul', said Shaka, 'woman and child'. He wanted nothing of Sikhunyana's to survive. The impi went in and finished them all off.

Mbokodo kaSikulekile

Although Sikhunyana had escaped – he died years later, an exile living in obscurity – the battle had been a crushing defeat for the Ndwandwe, who simply ceased to exist as an independent nation. Shaka's army marched in triumph back to Zululand, singing victory songs and driving its booty. After the ritual purification ceremonies, Shaka summoned it to Bulawayo once more, and judged its performance. Many heroes were rewarded, and the unfortunate cowards were picked out and executed beneath a bush which still stands, and is known as the *isihlahla samagwala*, 'the bush of cowards'. Fynn and his companions returned to Port Natal, rather chastened by this reminder of the realities of their position.

The Death of Nandi

The final defeat of the Ndwandwe secured Shaka's northern border,

and he began to look increasingly towards the south. Apart from the growing enclave at Port Natal, the area across the Thukela was disrupted as far as the amaMpondo kingdom 200 miles away. Beyond that lay the Xhosa, and the outposts of the mysterious subjects of King George on the Cape frontier. Shaka had raided the Mpondo several times, expeditions which had proved hugely profitable in cattle but which had failed to subjugate the kingdom itself. It seemed that, prompted by the Port Natal settlers, Shaka thought more and more about subduing the southern reaches and opening direct contact with the British. In November 1826 he moved his personal residence south of the Thukela and established an impressive new homestead at Dukuza, where the town of Stanger stands today. Whatever his long term aims, however, he was distracted at this point by personal tragedy.

Shaka had remained very close to his female relatives. Fynn had noticed his compassion towards his sick grandmother the year before, and his inconsolable grief when she died. In October 1827 Fynn was hunting elephant with the king when a messenger arrived with news that Nandi was ill. Shaka was devoted to his mother, a natural bond

According to Henry Francis Fynn, upon the death of Shaka's mother Nandi, her handmaidens were buried alive with her. Fynn's veracity has been questioned, but it seems likely that Nandi's death was the cause of considerable bloodshed.

37

exaggerated by the hardships they had shared as outcasts together, and he immediately abandoned the hunt and marched through the night to Mkhindini, Nandi's homestead about three miles from Bulawayo. Fynn was promptly ordered to attend her, but it was clear from the beginning that her condition was hopeless. She was dying of dysentery, and there was nothing he could do. He told the king as much, and Shaka withdrew into private thought until news came that Nandi was dead. Fynn described what happened next:

As soon as the death was announced publicly, the women and all the men who were present tore instantly from their persons every description of ornament. Shaka now appeared before the hut in which the body lay, surrounded by his principal Chiefs in their war attire. For about 20 minutes he stood in a silent mournful attitude with his head bowed upon his shield, and on which I saw large tears fall. After two or three deep sighs, his feelings becoming ungovernable, he broke out into frantic yells, which fearfully contrasted with the silence that had hitherto prevailed. This signal was enough. The Chiefs and people, to the number of about 15,000, commenced the most dismal and horrid lamentations.

The mass hysteria continued for several days, while Shaka strove to control his personal grief. Packed together and prevented by custom from eating or drinking, many of the people Fynn noted with horror, succumbed to exhaustion, while others began attacking one another in a frenzy of public despair. Fynn subsequently claimed that as many as 7,000 people died in the following week, a figure which has been challenged, and which does seem high, yet 'there was very general mourning on [Nandi's] account. Shaka himself cried. Many people were killed in mourning the *inkosikazi* [Queen]' (Jantshi kaNongila).

At last, Shaka called an end to the indiscriminate killing, but rigid prohibitions were placed on many aspects of everyday life for a period of national mourning. Failure to observe them was a capital offence. Wherever Shaka travelled about his kingdom, he orchestrated great public displays of grief.

After six months had elapsed, he held a purification ceremony to signal an end to the mourning. Ngomane kaMqoboli, his friend and adviser since his Mthethwa days, addressed the assembled nation and declared that the Mpondo had not shown sufficient respect for the king's distress. He demanded that this slight must be avenged. Clearly he was acting as the king's mouthpiece, and Shaka's mind had once more turned to his political goals, which were being presented to his subjects in personal terms, to maximize their sympathy.

The army was to be launched south.

Diplomatic Defeat

Shaka's campaign against the Mpondo in 1828 remains shrouded in

The site of Nandi's grave as it appears today.

mystery. That the Port Natal settlers were involved in some capacity is clear enough, but their own accounts are vague about their motives and actions. Clearly there was more to the expedition than a mere cattle raid, for no sooner had the army set off than Shaka announced his intention of sending a diplomatic mission to meet with the British at the Cape. It was to be led by several of his most trusted advisers and accompanied by representatives from the whites at Port Natal. According to Fynn and Isaacs – who left the only accounts written from Shaka's perspective that survive – the main purpose of the mission was to obtain for Shaka a cosmetic known as macassar oil. This was a hair oil that Fynn had casually mentioned one day, and which Shaka had seized upon and apparently believed contained the power to restore lost youth. The king had a dread of old age – 'when [he] got older he used to have the white hairs pulled out of his head, he always wanted to remain quite young' (Mayinga kaMbekuzana) – and may well have believed that this oil was a potent medicine. But there was clearly more to it than that. Some historians believe the traders had persuaded Shaka that the British would welcome his attack on the frontier peoples, hoping that any Anglo–Zulu alliance which followed would recognize their own commercial and territorial claims.

Whatever the reason, the combined diplomatic and military approach was a complete failure. The army moved south through Natal, looting and destroying any settlements it came across. The Mpondo abandoned their herds and retreated to their mountain strongholds, so

39

the Zulus rounded up the cattle and returned home. The diplomatic mission sailed to Port Elizabeth, but was prevented from reaching the administrative centre at Grahamstown. Because it came at the same time as an attack, the Colonial authorities suspected the whites' motives and believed the Zulus to be no more than spies. No official of any standing would grant them an audience, and they were detained for three months and carefully questioned. While they were there, a British force was sent out to the frontier, where it encountered a force believed to be Zulus. In fact, the Zulus had already withdrawn, and this force was the Ngwane of the marauder Matiwane, who had chosen this unfortunate moment to cross the Drakensberg from the interior. In two sharp battles the British dispersed them, and returned to the Colony convinced that they had trounced the mighty Shaka. Meanwhile the envoys had given up all hope of success, and begged to be allowed to return home. The Colonial officials were only too pleased to see them go.

The whole episode had been a farce. The army had not properly carried out its orders, the king's envoys had been rebuffed, and, to cap it all, the traders had forgotten Shaka's macassar oil. Shaka realized he had been made a fool of, and was furious. The traders scurried back to Port Natal to escape his wrath, and the army was sent on a new campaign to the north, without the customary lull to recover.

Yet this fresh campaign would prove a deadly misjudgement.

Assassination

It has been argued that King's Shaka's behaviour became unstable and erratic after the death of his mother. Certainly there had been something seriously wrong in the planning of the Mpondo campaign. The army, which had always been the basis of Shaka's power, was now disgruntled and it embarked on the fresh campaign reluctantly. Moreover the king's temper was more unpredictable than ever, and life at Dukuza was increasingly precarious. One particular atrocity was clearly remembered nearly a century later:

Shaka cut open a number of women when their husbands were away on campaign in order to see how the child lay in the womb. That was one of the reasons why Dingane put Shaka to death. These women had done no wrong.

Maziyana kaMahlabeni

The king was becoming dangerously isolated at court. Many of his advisers were away with the army and the whites had fallen from grace. His support amongst the Zulu people had waned. Circumstances were

ripe for a move against him, and, sure enough, one emerged. Shaka had always treated his half-brothers, Senzangakhona's sons by other wives, with respect, despite those who warned him that they posed a threat to his security. Two of his younger brothers, the Princes Dingane and Mhlangana, now conspired against him. They had apparently hatched a plot sometime before the launch of the new campaign, for both had feigned sickness and asked to be excused from duty with their regiments. Personal ambition was no doubt their main motive, but tradition credits Dingane with a genuine desire to free the people from Shaka's unpredictable tyranny.

Disposing of the king was no easy matter, however. The conspirators were terrified of being discovered, and were overawed by Shaka himself. Such was the daunting reputation and mystique of power the king had created around himself that few Zulus dared approach or look him in the eye, let alone attack him. To help them, the conspirators recruited one of Shaka's *izinceku*, or personal servants, Mbopha kaSitayi. Their chance came on the afternoon of 22 September 1828. Shaka left Dukuza to visit a small homestead nearby, where he was in the habit of receiving the stream of messengers who attended him almost daily from neighbouring peoples. On this occasion he was to meet a delegation of amaMpondo bearing a tribute of feathers and pelts, presumably a peace offering after the recent fighting. It was a routine audience, but it was to be dramatically interrupted:

41

Most accounts agree that Mbopha began the attack, bursting in upon the startled assembly and driving the Mpondo off with sticks. As the king stood up in astonishment, Mbopha, too scared to come close to him, threw a spear which wounded him. Shaka started to run towards the entrance of the homestead, when the two brothers vaulted a reed screen and intercepted him, stabbing him through and through. 'Sons of my father, what is wrong?' he cried, and then, as he fell, 'You will not rule when I am gone, for the land will see white people and locusts come!' He died in a pool of blood in the dust of the cattle kraal.

It is said that Mhlangana jumped over Shaka's body when he was dead, to assume his spiritual powers of kingship. It did him no good. There was no room for two claimants to the throne, and Dingane struck first. He had Mhlangana murdered, then sought out and destroyed Shaka's remaining supporters. By the time the army returned home, it found Dingane secure on the throne. The campaign had, in any case, been a disaster. The army had marched to the Limpopo River, where it had suffered heavily from disease and hunger. For once, their enemies had defeated them, and the Zulus straggled home in disarray. They were only too pleased to escape Shaka's wrath.

The conspirators had been too scared to bury Shaka's body, and it lay in the open all night, no one daring to touch it. There was to be no grand funeral, and no prolonged ceremony of mourning; at dawn the next day someone tumbled the corpse into an empty grain pit and sealed it with a stone.

Curiously, Shaka's dying prophecy seems to have come true. In 1829 Zululand was devastated by a plague of locusts. King Dingane proved a less vigorous leader than his half-brother, and he spent much of his early reign consolidating his power. He curried favour with the army by relaxing many of Shaka's harsher restrictions, and the warriors spent less time on duty in the amakhanda. As a result, power began to slip from the king's grasp, and the later history of the Zulu kingdom was characterized by a tension between the state apparatus and the clan system. Dingane's most significant problem, however, was posed by the influx of whites into Natal. In 1838 the vanguard of the Boer Great Trek reached Natal, which resulted in a costly war which shattered the Zulus at the battle of Blood River. Dingane himself was overthrown by another of Senzangakhona's sons, Mpande. The kingdom Shaka had forged survived for another forty years, to do battle with even more powerful interlopers, the British. The army, still basically the same organization created by Shaka, triumphed at Isandlwana in 1879, but collapsed beneath a hail of fire at Ulundi six months later.

The land had indeed seen white people come, and, like the locusts, they had left a swathe of destruction in their wake.

Today, Shaka's presence is still very much felt in Zululand. All trace of his great homestead at Dukuza has gone, submerged, almost symbolically, beneath the sprawling modern town of Stanger, but there is a handsome monument on the site of his grave, and nearby stands the boulder upon which he was sitting when attacked. A score of place-names associate him with local landmarks, some of them genuine – like a pile of stones high on a hillside, where he used to watch his army moving between Dukuza and nearby amakhanda – others more facile, like the Shaka's Rock beach resort. The Boers and the British failed to overturn his royal house, and the current king of the Zulus, His Majesty Goodwill Zwelithini, traces his ancestry to Senzangakhona and beyond. The anniversary of Shaka's death each year has become a national day for the Zulus, an opportunity for political parties to hold rallies and make speeches, for the Zulu role within the drama of contemporary South Africa is a complex one. Yet, however much his memory may have become political property, there is no doubt that King Shaka is a genuine source of pride and unity amongst the Zulus, even for those who, historically, were never part of the kingdom he created.

Whatever else may be said of his life, he had a remarkable spirit, and it lives on among his people.

Shaka's Army

It is difficult to be certain about the size of Shaka's army. Tradition has it that it was 400 strong when he first took control of the Zulu throne, and that it had grown to ten times that number by the battle of Gqokli two years later. Wild estimates suggest that it had reached 40,000 or even 60,000 by the height of his reign, but a more accepted figure, based on probable population figures, indicates that it probably never rose much above 15,000.

The role of the amabutho within Zulu society has already been considered. At regular intervals, every few years, the king would call up all young men who had reached their late teens, and form them into an ibutho. Each ibutho was given a name, and directed to build an ikhanda at an appointed place. In Shaka's time, it would remain in service there until he gave it permission to marry and disperse, but in the later years of the kingdom the warriors spent most of their time at home with their families, and reported to their ikhanda only when mustered for a particular duty. Military training formed an important part of the life of an ikhanda, but the warriors also spent much of their time tending the

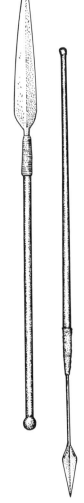

Shaka is credited with having invented the broad-bladed stabbing spear (left), which out-classed the existing throwing spear (right) in close-quarter fighting, and was undoubtedly a factor in the Zulu military success.

43

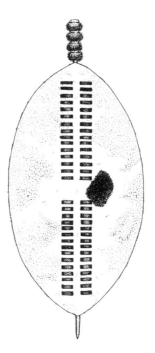

king's cattle, keeping the huts in good order, taking part in organized hunts, and attending various ceremonial gatherings.

Each ibutho was between 600 and 1,200 warriors strong, and divided into two wings, right and left, which were further subdivided into companies of between fifty and seventy men apiece. Company officers were elected by their comrades, but the high ranks – wing commanders, the regimental second-in-command and the commander-in-chief – were appointed by the king. For most of his reign, Shaka led the army in person, and it owed much of its success to his outstanding qualities as a general. Shaka's spy system was legendary, and he seldom embarked on a campaign without thoroughly assessing the strength, disposition and, if possible, intentions of his enemy. He was an able strategist and an inspired tactician, a ruthless and aggressive commander who was never afraid to strike hard and fast, and who had an instinctive grasp of fieldcraft which enabled him to turn the terrain to his advantage. When, in later years, he no longer took to the field himself, he shared his plans with only his most trusted commanders.

Each ibutho had a distinctive uniform, consisting of feathers, pelts, and the colour on the face of the war-shield. The king carefully sorted his cattle according to the colour of their hides before distributing them among his regiments. Each ibutho was allotted a particular colour, and, in due course, the hides from these beasts would be used to make war-shields. These shields were not the property of individual warriors, but were kept in special stores within the amakhanda. The war-shield of Shaka's day was about five feet tall, and two feet six inches wide, with a

44

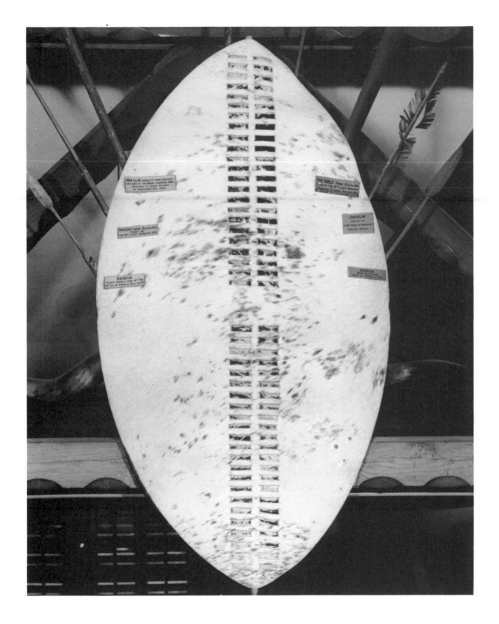

stout stick at the back, held in place by two rows of parallel hide lacing. The top of the stick was wound round with a strip of decorative fur. As a general rule, the youngest regiments carried black shields, the number and size of white patches rising with experience, until senior regiments carried all-white shields. Red, dun-coloured and speckled grey (white and black hairs intermixed) shields were also carried. In Shaka's time, the difference between the various regimental shield patterns could be quite subtle, but were considered of the greatest importance.

Everyday male dress consisted of a thin belt of hide around the waist, with an oblong of soft cowhide over the buttocks, and strips of fur,

Splendid, full-sized war shield of a type known as isihlangu, *introduced in Shaka's day and still carried in the 1879 Anglo–Zulu War, where this example was taken. (English Heritage / Osborne House: photo by Frank Taylor).*

twisted together to resemble animal tails, dangling at the front. In addition, however, each ibutho had a sumptuous dress uniform. The bushy parts of cows' tails were worn in profusion, suspended from a necklace so as to hang in bunches to the waist at the front and the knees behind, or from thongs around the elbows and knees, wrists and ankles. Some senior regiments wore an ornate kilt which encircled the waist with twisted tails of genet- and monkey-skin. A stuffed headband of otter- or leopard-skin formed the basis of the headdress, with earflaps of monkey-skin dangling over the cheeks. Each regiment had its own particular combination of feathers in the headdress. Young regiments wore the long glossy black tail feathers of the *sakabuli* bird on either side of the head, or on top of it, while senior regiments wore one or two blue crane feathers. Black-and-white ostrich feathers were worn in different arrangements, and the king himself often granted permission for a regiment to wear a particular plume, in recognition of some special service. Only a few individual heroes could wear the waxy red and green tail feathers of the loury. Much of this costume was ex-

46

tremely fragile and expensive, and in later years it was only worn on ceremonial occasions, but the evidence of Fynn and others suggests that at least some of it was worn into battle in Shaka's day.

When the king summoned the army for a campaign, the amabutho were expected to march from their amakhanda and assemble at the capital within a few days. There they would undergo various cere-

Items of Zulu warrior's costume in the Natal Museum, Pietermaritzburg: a cheetah-fur headband (right), and a headress of sakabuli feathers (top), typically worn by junior regiments.

47

monies designed to bind them together and bring ruin on their enemies. They would march off in columns preceded by a screen of scouts. For the first few days they would be accompanied by boys too young to fight, who carried the sleeping mats of the most important warriors and drove cattle for slaughter. After that, the warriors would have to survive by foraging. The mobility of the Zulu army is well known, and daily marches of twenty or thirty miles over rugged country were commonplace. When they drew near the enemy, if time permitted, they would be formed into a circle and given their orders. Once an attack had begun, it was seldom possible for the izinduna to recall it, and it usually resulted in victory or flight. After a successful battle enemy dead were mutilated in accordance with superstitious ritual, friendly dead would be carried off by friends and relatives, and the wounded treated with herbal potions by traditional healers. When the campaign ended, the warriors would then undergo a period of post-combat purification rites, and be called before the king to account for themselves in the recent fight.

Today, the founder of the Zulu nation lies buried beneath Couper Street, in the town of Stanger, which has obliterated all trace of his Dukuza homestead. This monument is thought to mark the site.

Bibliography

The historiography of pre-Colonial black South Africa is currently the subject of much critical debate, and King Shaka, perhaps more than any other nineteenth-century black leader, is in desperate need of a reassessment. The only full-length biography of him, E.A. Ritter's *Shaka Zulu* (1955), is heavily fictionalized, and by no means all more modern works avoid the pitfalls. Much has been written about Shaka, but most of it should be treated with caution. The following books remain important reading, however:

Byant, A.T. *Olden Times in Zululand and Natal*, 1929.
Fynn, H.F. *The Diary of Henry Francis Fynn*, edited by J. Stuart and McK. D. Malcolm, 1950.
Gray, Stephen (ed) *The Natal Papers of 'John Ross'*, 1992.
Isaacs, Nathanial *Travels and Adventures in East Africa*; 2 vols, 1936.
Omer-Cooper, J.D. *The Zulu Aftermath*, 1966.

Zulu accounts are to be found in *The James Stuart Archive*, edited by C. de B. Webb and J. Wright; 4 vols, 1976, 1979, 1982 and 1986. Louis du Buisson's *The White Man Cometh* (1989) is an attempt to dispel the myths early white adventurers created around their activities and their relationship with Shaka, while Charles Ballard's *The House of Shaka* (1988) is the first attempt at a complete history of the Zulu royal house. T.V. Bulpin's *Shaka's Country* (1952) is an anecdotal but appealing history of the Zulu kingdom. J.S. and A.P. Bergh's *Tribes and Kingdoms* (1984) is a useful introduction to the period.

Chronology

In the absence of written sources, it is not always possible to fix pre-Colonial dates with certainty. Those given here, particularly the early ones, must therefore be regarded as approximate only.

1787	Shaka born.
1805	Shaka joins Mthethwa army.
1816	Shaka succeeds to the chieftainship of the Zulu.
1817	Dingiswayo killed by Zwide.
1818	APRIL Battle of Gqokli Hill; first defeat of Ndwandwe.
1819	Battle of Mhlatuze; second defeat of Ndwandwe.
1819	Shaka builds his great Bulawayo homestead, overlooking the Mhlatuze valley.
1819–24	Period of increased Zulu raiding activity.
1824	MAY First white traders arrive at Port Natal.
1826	Ndwandwe invasion; battle of Ndolowane Hill.
1826	NOVEMBER Shaka builds his Dukuza homestead, south of the Thukela.
1827	OCTOBER Nandi, Shaka's mother, dies.
1828	Expedition against the amaMpondo.
1828	22 SEPTEMBER Shaka assassinated.

Moshoeshoe

OF THE BASOTHO

Moshoeshoe as King of the Basotho in 1833. Perhaps a little romanticised, this is the earliest portrait and is based upon Casalis' description. In later life, Moshoeshoe preferred to be depicted in European dress

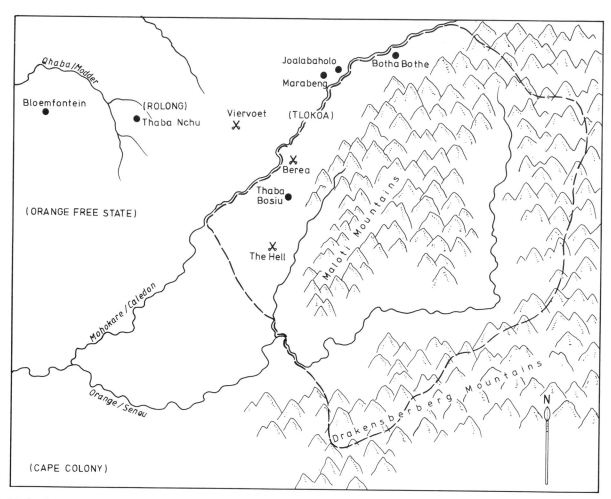

Qhaba/Modder

Bloemfontein

(ROLONG)
Thaba Nchu

Viervoet

Joalabaholo

Marabeng

Botha Bothe

(TLOKOA)

(ORANGE FREE STATE)

Berea

Thaba
Bosiu

Mohokare/Caledon

The Hell

Maloti Mountains

Orange/Senqu

Drakensberg Mountains

N

(CAPE COLONY)

*Moshoeshoe's Basotho king-
dom, shown at the height of
his power. His influence extended from the Orange River
in the south, to Thaba Nchu
in the west. The dotted line
marks the boundary of
BaSotholand upon incorpora-
tion into the Cape Colony in
1871.*

When I was a young man, I had a great desire to become a chief. I longed that my chieftainship should grow and rise . . .

(Moshoeshoe, recalling his ambitions)

His eyes, full of softness and intelligence, made a deep impression on me. I felt I had to do with a superior man, trained to think, to command others, and above all himself.

(Eugene Casalis' description of Moshoeshoe)

Chief by the Grace of the People

At first glance, there are a number of similarities between the careers of King Moshoeshoe of the BaSotho and his more famous contemporary, King Shaka of the Zulu. Both were the sons of minor chiefs, both achieved some early fame as warriors, both owed their rise to a period of terrible upheaval and both emerged as the founding fathers of new nation-states. Yet their personalities had little in common.

Shaka was a ruthless warrior who exploited a period of tension to expand his territory by the vigorous use of military force. The resulting Zulu kingdom was politically highly centralized, with the king himself keeping a tight grip on the reigns of power. Moshoeshoe, on the other hand, was a statesman; a compassionate man who accumulated followers by offering them refuge on his mountain stronghold, and demanding allegiance, rather than submission, in return. His followers regarded him with respect rather than awe. Throughout his reign, the BaSotho were torn by internal dissension and threatened by external aggression, yet Moshoeshoe held his kingdom together, and his legacy today is the independent Kingdom of Lesotho.

What type of man was he? His physical appearance is well known, since he was photographed several times later in his life – he lived more than forty years longer than Shaka. He was a man of above average height, bearded, with a face that suggests both authority and humanity, and a dignity that is not diminished by the incongruous European clothes he habitually wore during audiences with whites. We have no descriptions of him as a young man, for it was not until June 1833 that French protestant missionaries left the first written portrait of him. Eugene Casalis' account pictures him in the prime of life, and approaching the height of his power and influence:

His profile, much more aquiline than the generality of his subjects, his well-developed forehead, the fullness and regularity of his features, his eyes, a little weary, as it seemed, but full of intelligence and softness, made a deep impression on me. I felt at once that I had to do with a superior man, trained to think, to command others, and above all himself.

He appeared to be about forty-five years of age. The upper part of his body, entirely naked, was perfectly modelled, sufficiently fleshy, but without obesity. I admired the graceful line of his

53

shoulders and the fineness of his hand. He had allowed to fall round him, from his middle, a large mantle of panther skins as lissom as the finest cloth, and the folds of which covered his knees and his feet. For sole ornament he had bound to his forehead a string of glass beads, to which was fastened a tuft of feathers, which floated behind the neck. He wore on his right arm a bracelet of ivory – an emblem of power – and some copper rings on his wrists.

Intelligence and compassion – these were qualities that struck many of the European missionaries, soldiers and farmers who met Moshoeshoe. Only those who coveted his land had cause to complain of his implacable opposition. In return, Moshoeshoe admired and respected whites, though he was not prepared to sacrifice the best interests of his people to them. Initially, he took the lofty rhetoric and idealism proffered by those who called themselves Christians at face value. Later, when he discovered that fine words masked hypocrisy and greed, he was to be bitterly disillusioned. Nevertheless, though he came to realize that their needs were often diametrically opposed to his own, Moshoeshoe tried to deal with the whites fairly and sympathetically. Though he was not above waging war when it was necessary, he abhorred it, believing that 'peace is the rain which makes the grass grow, while war is like the wind which dries it up'.

Of the nature of his internal rule, the missionary Arbousset has left a glowing account:

In everything this African prince has shown a tact which I admire extremely. His affability has not flagged for a single moment. Vivacity, gaiety, nothing is lacking in him. He speaks to anyone without regard to age or rank. He even amuses himself with the children, as if he were one of them himself; and, even more astonishing, his memory is so good that he seems to know the name and history of each of his subjects. I leave it to the imagination whether, with such qualities, he is popular among them!

Certainly Moshoeshoe preferred to rule his people by consensus whenever possible, leading them subtly round to his own way of thinking in the *pitso*, the tribal gathering where Sotho men discussed events of national importance. Arbousset commented that 'Be it principle with him, or be it habit, he is long in speaking, vague, too subject to digressions; a word which he lets fall here and there often reveals his true thought, and it is only the cleverest among his people who grasp it.' Not that he was a paragon of virtues, for when sorely tried he had a fearsome temper that few dared to cross. Arbousset, again captures a moment of fury when a legal dispute Moshoeshoe was judging got out of hand:

On both sides people get hot and excited; one of the friends of the widow takes her part and speaks rather lengthily in her favour, when suddenly Moshoeshoe violently throws a stone at him, hurls himself across the crowd, batters his body and tries to kill him, which he would have done except for some friends of the wretch who pull him from his clutches and drag him outside.

No doubt, trying to rule the BaSotho in such difficult times could be an extremely frustrating business, and such outbursts were only to be

expected. Despite them, Moshoeshoe is remembered as 'a man who loved people', and one who most aptly fulfilled the Sotho proverb encapsulating the ideal relationship between the ruler and his subjects – 'A chief is a chief by the grace of the people'.

BaSotho chief: rank and prestige were indicated by a cloak of leopardskin – and by a curious metal breastplate, worn suspended from a thong around the neck.

The Sotho World

Moshoeshoe was born about 1786, in the village of Menkhoaneng on the banks of the Hlotse River, in the eastern high veld of central southern Africa. The southern tip of the great continent rises steadily from the Atlantic coast in the west, reaching a tableland between 6,000 and 10,000 feet high where it abuts the spectacular rampart of the Drakensberg mountains, which cut off the eastern coastal strip and shaped the age-old spread of human population. Beyond the Drakensberg, moving through the coastal downlands, filtered the cultural and linguistic group known as the Nguni, while the plateau of the interior was the home of the Sotho people. Although closely related, and sharing many similar customs, the languages of the two groups were mutually unintelligible, and interaction between them was limited, since the Drakensberg could only be crossed at a few difficult passes. The Sotho were mixed farmers whose staple crop was sorghum, and for whom, like the Nguni, cattle represented a means of assessing wealth and regulating all social relationships. They lived in clusters of dome-shaped thatch huts housing between fifty and several hundred people, each one ruled by a hereditary chief. Although many villages were linked by ties of kinship or allegiance, there was no larger political grouping than the chiefdom, and each chief's power was limited by his ability to maintain the support of his followers. Moshoeshoe's father, Mokhachane, was chief of the Bamokoteli. (In SeSotho, the Sotho language, the letter 'l' is pronounced *d* when followed by 'i'). They were a small subsection of a Sotho group known as the Bakoena (the people of the *koena*), after the crocodile, an animal that had a mystical significance for them.

For the Nguni, the coast offered at least an accidental chance of contact with the outside world, but until the 1820s the Sotho remained largely isolated, scarcely aware of the existence of the white race, interacting only with their neighbours. The economic repercussions of white settlement at the Cape had perhaps begun to affect trading and work patterns, and bands of dispossessed Kora had drifted north into the lands of the Sotho, but physical contact with whites themselves was probably nonexistent. Land was still plentiful, and the population had not yet risen to the levels necessary to force it into conflict with its environment. Friction between villages was common, as young warriors sought to prove their manhood by enriching themselves at the expense of their neighbours, but by common consent fighting was kept to a minimum. A far greater cause of tension was the supernatural, for the Sotho believed both that their ancestral spirits watched over their daily lives, and that they were vulnerable to virulent forms of witchcraft, which could only be detected through the agency of the diviners, *lingaka*. When Moshoeshoe was born he was named Lepoqo, meaning 'Dispute', reflecting a wrangle over accusations of witchcraft which was afflicting his village at the time.

The Young Warrior

Lepoqo's childhood was apparently a happy one. Years later, travelling about his kingdom in the company of the French missionaries, he pointed out to them the ruins of the village where he grew up, and they were surprised to see how affected he was on recognizing the hills and gullies where he had run and played as a boy. When he approached puberty, his father, as a chief, would have called a *lebollo*, a gathering of youths from his territory who were ready to be initiated into manhood.

Sotho warrior, in traditional dress, taken from Casalis' memoirs. The winged shield and hide cape are characteristic, whilst the flattened metal breastplate was worn only by senior warriors. The tall plume on the shield served as a rallying point in battle.

The initiation ceremonies were a crucial part of Sotho life. A bull captured from a rival village had to be slaughtered and doctored to convey its strength to the initiates, who were sprinkled with ritual potions in order of strict seniority in the *khotla*, the meeting place of the chief's court. They then had to spend between three and six months in the seclusion of the circumcision lodge, enduring the surgeon's knife, observing taboos and composing praise-poems to ensure their standing in adult life. Young Lepoqo assumed the name *Letlama*, 'the Binder', from the way he intended to bind and overpower his enemies, and his age-group took the name *Matlama*, 'the Binders'. The bonds linking fellow initiates were very great and would last throughout life. The Sotho had no standing army, but individual warriors expected their age-mates to support them on raiding forays and, on those rare occasions when the chiefdom itself was threatened, the age-groups fought together as loose tactical units.

As a young man, Moshoeshoe had none of his later qualms about waging war, and in fact earned a reputation as a skilful and daring warrior. Raiding cattle from rival clans was one way for a young warrior to enrich himself and build up a reputation. Such raids were usually carried out by a few adventurous individuals acting on their own initiative, who travelled fast, making the most of the terrain, hoping to catch their enemy by surprise and sweep away his cattle before he could muster to oppose them. Young warriors were duty bound to hand over much of their loot to their chiefs, but even so Moshoeshoe's success was such that he soon accumulated a moderate herd and attracted followers of his own. One raid was so profitable that it earned him a new name; he returned with so much booty from a chief named RaMonaheng that he was said to have shaved off the chief's beard – Moshoeshoe, pronounced *Mo-shwe-shwe*, recalls the swish of the razor.

About 1810 he secured his adult status by taking his first wife, and the next year his son Letsie was born. It was a happy marriage, but in accordance with Sotho custom he was to marry many times. At the height of his power the missionaries conjectured with disgust that he had as many as two hundred wives. Only the first three wives, though, were considered important – each of these had her own establishment and from their houses would come his heirs. His junior wives were regarded as little more than domestic servants.

Despite his prosperity Moshoeshoe remained ambitious, and the largely static Sotho society offered little opportunity for him to make his mark. As he himself later admitted:

When I was a young man, I had a great desire to become a chief. I longed that my chieftainship should grow and rise, and with this wish I went to see Mohlomi, whose chieftainship had been a great success . . . I asked him to advise me on how I could become a chief. Could it be by a charm?

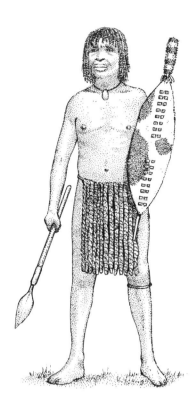

It is difficult now to sift the truth about Mohlomi from the layers of legend that surround him. Certainly he existed, a chief of the neighbouring Monaheng people, who was renowned as a traveller, and a man of visions and rare wisdom. In Moshoeshoe's story he has come to assume a similar role as Chief Dingiswayo does in the career of Shaka; a patron and mentor whose support and ideas provided a framework upon which his protégé could build. Certainly Mohlomi's words would have a profound effect on Moshoeshoe, highlighted as they were by the horrors to come – 'Go, rule by love, and look upon thy people as men and brothers'.

About 1820 Moshoeshoe felt confident enough to leave his father's village, taking with him his personal followers and many of the Matlama, and establish his own settlement. For his new home he chose a flat-topped mountain named Botha-Bothe, one of many similar plateaux that characterize the region, isolated outcrops cut adrift by river valleys and erosion, their summits surrounded by almost impenetrable layers of cliff. Some of his councillors questioned the wisdom of such a move, pointing out that hitherto only the despised San (bushmen) hunters had lived in caves or on the mountain tops, but Moshoeshoe's decision was to prove inspired. Mohlomi, it was said, had once had a dream full of terrible portents for the future, and he prophesied a dark age looming for the Sotho; 'After my death, a cloud

Hlubi warrior in the 1820s. The Hlubi were one of the two powerful groups coming from the coastal belt – the other was Matiwane's amaNgwane – who spread the disruption of the mfecane into the interior. Exact details of their appearance is obscure, but apparently they had a distinctive hair-style, and wore long loin-coverings of twisted goatskin. Their weapons were of the Nguni type, but these were probably smaller than the more famous Zulu styles.

59

of red dust will come out of the east and consume our tribes. The father will eat his children.'

Even as Moshoeshoe moved to Botha-Bothe, events were occurring beyond the Drakensberg that would make Mohlomi's vision come tragically true.

Red Dust from the East

In the congested coastal strip, the Nguni clans were collapsing in on one another like a falling house of cards. The process had begun long before Shaka had seized the throne of the Zulu in 1816, and by 1820 it was in full flow. The Sotho knew little of it beyond the stories told by a handful of refugees who crossed the mountain passes, and when the blow fell on them it was all the more terrible for being unexpected.

The agents of destruction were two powerful Nguni clans living in the foothills of the eastern slopes of the Drakensberg, along the upper reaches of the Mzinyathi and Thukela rivers – the Hlubi of Chief Mthimkhulu and the Ngwane of Chief Matiwane. The Hlubi had already been torn apart by a civil war, and Mthimkhulu's brother Mpangazitha had crossed into the high veld and settled on land owned by the Tlokoa Sotho. The Tlokoa were a large and powerful group ruled by a formidable lady named Queen 'MaNthatisi, on behalf of her under-age son, Sekonyela. The Hlubi were known to the Tlokoa who had traded across the passes, and 'MaNthatisi was content to allow Mpangazitha temporary use of some of her grazing land. Meanwhile Matiwane and Mthimkhulu were engaged in a bitter dispute over some cattle that Matiwane had lodged for safe keeping with Mthimkhulu, but which were not returned as agreed. Matiwane attacked the Hlubi, killed Mthimkhulu, and drove his followers over the mountains, where they joined Mpangazitha. No sooner had he done so than Matiwane himself was attacked by the Zulus and forced to flee into the high veld. The Ngwane fell once more on the Hlubi, seized their cattle and chased them away from their crops. The Hlubi in turn crashed into 'MaNthatisi's Tlokoa. Her warriors, with their light spears and shields, were no match for the invaders, who had adopted at least some of Shaka's revolutionary close-quarter fighting techniques. 'MaNthatisi collected her followers and fled, a horde of hungry men, women and children who, cut off from their own sources of food, had no choice but to attack anyone who lay in their path, plundering grain stores and looting cattle.

And so the terrible marauding that became known as *mfecane*, 'the crushing', spread to the high veld, where it is still known today under

the SeSotho version of the same word, the *lifaqane*. The predatory wanderings and their attendant disturbances would last until 1836, destroying dozens of independent chiefdoms and subjecting thousands to the horrors of war and famine. Order and discipline were swept away as some areas were completely depopulated, while in others the few wretched survivors were forced to turn to cannibalism to sustain themselves. In 1833 Casalis found plenty of evidence of the turmoil:

> We found on our track terrible indications of massacres and devastations. Almost everywhere were human bones. In some places their numbers indicated battlefields. Broken earthenware, fallen walls overgrown with brambles, the easily recognised boundaries of fields formerly cultivated revealed to us frequently that we were on the site of a once prosperous village. There were still some left which were inhabited, but they were much smaller and on almost inaccessible heights.

For a while Moshoeshoe and the Mokoteli went unmolested, but between 1822 and 1824 they suffered a series of raids from both Matiwane and the Tlokoa. For all Moshoeshoe's reputation as a warrior, he could not hope to compete against such overwhelming foes, and each time only Botha-Bothe's strong position saved him. Yet his power depended on his ability to feed his followers, and the raids left him impoverished and vulnerable. Clearly Botha-Bothe was too near the eye of the hurricane, and early in 1824 he sent out scouts to search for a new stronghold. They returned with reports of a suitable mountain about fifty-five

A study of a Tswana warrior by G.H. Ford. The Tswana were a western branch of the Sotho, and their military traditions were similar to those of the Sotho. For all this man's impressive array of weapons, the Sotho/Tswana were no match for either the Nguni or Kora.

61

miles to the southwest, in a large uninhabited area hitherto beyond the range of the marauders. In June or July 1824 Moshoeshoe and his people migrated.

Circling wide of the Tlokoa, Moshoeshoe led the Mokoteli on a long and difficult route that hugged the mountain foothills, plunging through narrow and dangerous passes, and winding past great jagged outcrops of rock. Though the distance was not great, progress was slow, for the people were weakened by hunger, and children and old folk lagged behind. Suddenly, as they crossed a particularly hazardous stretch, a band of cannibals burst from the rocks and dragged off several of the stragglers, including Moshoeshoe's grandfather, Peete. When the warriors rallied and rushed to their aid, they found nothing but a pile of bloodstained clothing. There was nothing to do but go on, and a few days later they arrived at the foot of the mountain that was to be their new home. It was late afternoon by the time they climbed the main pass to the summit, and as the sun sank on the horizen the rampart of cliffs seemed to grow higher in the lengthening shadows. The Bamokoteli gave the mountain a new name – *Thaba Bosiu*, 'the Mountain of Night'.

The Mountain is My Mother

Since Thaba Bosiu was to feature so strongly in Moshoeshoe's story, it is worth pausing to describe it in detail. Situated in a basin of hills, it was a completely isolated outcrop rising about four hundred feet from the valley of the Phuthiatsana River. Shaped roughly like a four-pointed star, the flat summit covered an area of less than two square miles, and was surrounded by walls of sandstone cliff averaging fifty feet in height. These were impenetrable except for six distinct passes, where fissures in the rock had left steep, narrow paths to the top. The summit was well-watered, and the grass there was sufficient to support a large herd of cattle for some weeks. There was little room to plant crops, but the surrounding valleys were extremely fertile, and those who settled there could be quickly moved on to the summit when danger threatened.

Moshoeshoe marked out his new territory with a practised eye. For his own village he chose a site within a quarter of a mile of the principal pass, known as the Khubelu or RaFutho. The other passes were allocated between members of his family to guard. He ordered that piles of stones be heaped along the crest of each one, so that they could be rolled down on any attacker trying to climb up. By the time his preparations were complete, Thaba Bosiu was virtually impregnable to any military technology lacking explosives, and, indeed, it was never

stormed in his lifetime, even by European armies armed with artillery.

To survive on the mountain, Moshoeshoe needed cattle to attract and support followers. Not long after his arrival he organized the first of a series of spectacularly successful raids which swept down through the Drakensberg passes and carried off thousands of cattle belonging to the Thembu chieftains there. Sure enough, word soon spread about his apparent power and prosperity, and refugees from the *lifaqane* began to make their way towards Thaba Bosiu. Moshoeshoe accepted them all willingly. Dispossessed individuals or small groups were distributed among his existing followers, while any chiefs who came to him with their people were allowed to retain their position so long as they acknowledged his authority. Any who had cattle gave them up to the national herd, but were loaned them back under the *mafisa* system, in which the state retained technical ownership but allowed its subjects the use of them. Herds plundered in raids were usually distributed in the same way. Moshoeshoe's son Sekhonyana testified to the success of these methods:

[Moshoeshoe] gained the esteem of the [BaSotho] and established his power by succouring the distressed and protecting them and not keeping recaptured cattle of other clans of the [BaSothos] for himself, as he could have done according to custom, but returning them to their owners.

Thaba Bosiu, showing Khubelu Pass, one of the main passes up to the summit. The building on top of the mountain, to the right, is Moshoeshoe's European-style house; whilst the mission station is on the left.

Within a few years his following had grown to such an extent that he was known not merely as a *Morena*, a Chief, but as a *Morena e Moholo*, a Great Chief, or King. His people began to stop referring to themselves as Mokoteli or the countless other group names reflecting their origins, but called themselves instead simply *BaSotho*, 'the Sotho People'.

Survival of the Nation

Unfortunately, such a haven of peace and plenty brought with it a considerable risk, looking ever more tempting as it did to the high veld war lords. The Tlokoa had ceased wandering and established their own mountain retreats at Marabeng and Joalaboholo forty miles to the north, and Matiwane had decisively smashed the Hlubi and killed Mpangazitha in 1825. However, the Ngwane chief's settlements were creeping westwards, and by 1826 one of his outposts was only eight miles from Thaba Bosiu. Moshoeshoe tried to ensure his safety by paying Matiwane *nyehelo*, a tribute of cattle which implied submission, but the existence of the two groups in the same vicinity was bound to lead to friction. In February 1828 Matiwane, urged on by his councillors (who regarded Moshoeshoe as a Sotho upstart and yearned for his cattle), launched his warriors against Thaba Bosiu.

Moshoeshoe, reluctant to risk a prolonged siege on the mountain top, decided to chance a battle in the open, and drew up his forces at the foot of the Khubelu pass. The Ngwane advanced swiftly to the attack, and to Moshoeshoe's horror the Sotho broke. The Ngwane got in amongst them, stabbing right and left with their spears. One warrior skewered a light Sotho shield and held it up calling out in contempt 'Look at this shield! Whose little shield is this!'. At that point Moshoeshoe unleashed his reserve, his own Matlama regiment, and the fresh assault caught the Ngwane off guard. Their attack stalled and they were driven back, finally abandoning their weapons and fleeing with the jubilant Sotho in pursuit.

Matiwane's defeat was a turning point in the history of the high veld. Though his power was by no means broken, he was becoming increasingly unhappy in his territory. He had found to his cost that he was still within range of Zulu raids, and now Moshoeshoe was also proving a threat. He decided to migrate once more back across the Drakensberg, but his timing was unfortunate. He arrived east of the Cape frontier in the aftermath of a Zulu expedition and blundered into British patrols who mistook him for Shaka. In July and August 1828 he was severely defeated in two sharp battles, and his power was broken. For a while he wandered through Moshoeshoe's territory, and the

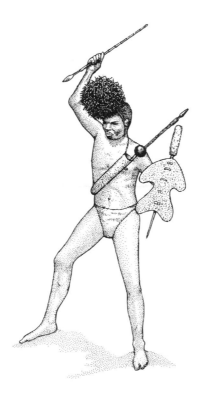

Sotho king magnanimously offered him sanctuary, but he was determined to return to his homeland on the Thukela River. He arrived after Shaka's assassination, and when he sought to pay his respects to Shaka's successor, Dingane, the Zulu king had him executed.

The comprehensive destruction of the Ngwane left Moshoeshoe unchallenged in the southern high veld, but his problems were by no means over. His authority was spreading steadily out from Thaba Bosiu, absorbing lesser chiefdoms, and clearing up the debris of the *lifaqane*. Several thousand cannibals still infested the region, and Moshoeshoe, despite the revulsion his subjects felt at their crimes, tried to lure them back to more normal society and rehabilitate them. Among those brought in were the very band who had eaten his grandfather Peete; the Sotho clamoured for them to be put to death but, in a famous judgement, Moshoeshoe argued that, as the living tombs of his ancestors, they could not be harmed. The grateful cannibals were given cattle and set free, and were gradually absorbed within the ranks of the BaSotho.

As his boundaries expanded, however, Moshoeshoe faced new threats from bands of Kora horsemen in the west, and from the emergent Ndebele kingdom based along the Apies and Crocodile rivers in the far north. The Kora (or Korana) were the descendants of the Khoikhoi, the original inhabitants of the Cape, who had been pushed farther and farther north as white settlement there increased. They had

Ordinary Sotho warrior from the 1820s. The winged shield, ostrich-feather headress, breach-hide and quiver of spears were common to most of the Sotho and Tswana (western Sotho) groups of the interior. The BaSotho retained this style of dress until it was gradually eroded by their contact with Europeans in the mid-nineteenth century.

adopted European clothing, horses and guns, and lived a semi-nomadic existence on the northern Cape frontier, subsisting by hunting and banditry. They used their horses and guns to terrify and kill local tribesmen and to plunder their herds. The Kora had crossed the Cape's boundary, the Orange (Senqu) River, early in the nineteenth century, moving north into the dry plains to the west of the BaSotho territory. From about 1825 Moshoeshoe received a string of reports from his outlying districts detailing Kora depredations. Restless and lawless, the Kora were difficult to deal with, rejecting Moshoeshoe's overtures, on one occasion killing the messengers who brought them a peace offering. Reluctantly, Moshoeshoe sanctioned the use of force, and one Kora band was surrounded during the night and butchered almost to a man at dawn. But still the sporadic attacks continued, for their weapons gave the Kora an undeniable advantage during daylight fighting. The Kora problem was to plague Moshoeshoe for nearly a decade, and was only to be resolved when the tide of white expansion pushed the bandits on once more, beyond the Sotho borders.

The Ndebele threat was greater, but more decisively resolved. The Ndebele were the followers of Mzikilazi, a general serving Shaka who had broken away from the Zulus and moved into the interior to establish his own kingdom. By 1830 he had established a secure base in what is now the central Transvaal. In 1831 he sent a force on a raiding expedition to attack the Tlokoa, now ruled by Sekonyela, who had reached adulthood. Sekonyela regarded Moshoeshoe as a rival, and they were to clash frequently over the years, but on this occasion he sent a message to Moshoeshoe to warn him of the Ndebele approach. It was well timed, for the Ndebele apparently decided against storming Marabeng, and drifted south, looking for easier prey. Moshoeshoe hastily gathered his people on Thaba Bosiu and strengthened his defences, believing that, unlike Matiwane, the Ndebele were too far from home to risk a prolonged siege. He was right. The Ndebele arrived sometime in March, and moved to attack straight away, deploying their regiments at the foot of five of the six passes. Casalis, who probably heard the story of the battle from participants only two years later, describes what happened next:

Nothing seemed to arrest the rush of the enemy. Accustomed to victory the [Ndebele] advanced in serried ranks, not appearing to observe the masses of basalt which came rolling down with a tremendous noise from the top of the mountain. But soon there was a general crush – an irresistible avalanche of stones, accompanied by a shower of javelins, sent back the assailants with more rapidity than they had advanced. The chiefs might then be seen rallying the fugitives; and snatching away the plumes with which their heads were decorated, and trampling them under foot in rage, would lead their men again towards the formidable rampart. This desperate attempt succeeded no better than the former one. The blow was decisive.

There is a story that, as the Ndebele withdrew, Moshoeshoe sent after them a messenger with a gift of cattle and the words '[Moshoeshoe] salutes you. Supposing that hunger has brought you into this country, he sends you these cattle, that you may eat them on the way home.' If true – and it was a ploy Moshoeshoe certainly used on other occasions – it was an act of calculated humility which allowed the Ndebele to save face and offered peace for the future. For whatever reason, Mzilikazi did not attack the BaSotho again.

The Missionaries

By the early 1830s the Sotho kingdom was relatively secure. Matiwane was gone, the Ndebele were repulsed, the Tlokoa were quiet, and only the Kora were a constant source of aggravation. Yet history was poised to introduce a new factor, and the threat to Moshoeshoe would be as great as anything he had experienced before.

Until that time, there is no record of a white man ever having travelled through LeSotho (the land of the Sotho). No doubt Moshoeshoe would have heard of the existence of Europeans from the African hunters who moved between the Cape and the vast game herds that inhabited the interior, and perhaps some of his own subjects would have taken advantage of the more settled times to go in search of work in the Colony. But the first white men we can be sure he met were a party of Afrikaner (Boer) hunters who passed through his lands in June 1831. Moshoeshoe begged them to help him in his struggle against the Kora, but they were reluctant to become involved in local feuds. But the idea had taken root in the king's mind, and when a Christian Griqua named Adam Krotz visited him towards the end of 1832 and raised the subject of missionaries, Moshoeshoe seized his opportunity:

The idea of having near him permanently wise men, friends of peace, disposed to do all in their power to aid him in his distress, pleased him greatly. He wanted to have some at once. 'Do you know any?' he said to me, 'who would be disposed to come?' I replied that such men sometimes came our way. 'Oh, I beseech you, tell the first you meet to hasten here. I will give them the best possible welcome. I will do everything they advise me to do.' I promised him not to forget his prayer.

Krotz did not forget, and the message of an African kingdom yearning to be enlightened filtered back through missionary channels. In June 1833 two missionaries from the Paris Evangelical Mission, Thomas Arbousset and Eugene Casalis, together with their assistant Gosselin, arrived in a trek-wagon at Thaba Bosiu, and a historic meeting took place. Moshoeshoe was delighted to see him, and gave them permission to erect a mission on his land. 'I have been told that you can help us. You promise to do it. It is enough. It is all I want to know!' he cried.

And so began Moshoeshoe's long involvement with the missionaries. His desire to learn both spiritual and earthly wisdom cannot be denied.

He listened carefully to their Christian teachings, finding much that agreed with his own views on love, harmony and equality. He was impressed by their clothes, wagon and tools, and declared that the Sotho were woefully lacking in intelligence compared to the Europeans. Yet the missionaries offered him much more, an access to another world which he foresaw was stronger than his own, and which he could not hope to understand unaided. He remained on close personal terms with Arbousset, but in Casalis he found a true friend. The two instinctively understood one another, and Moshoeshoe came increasingly to rely on him as an adviser, translator and confidant. Years later an anonymous missionary would write enthusiastically in the *South African Commercial Advertiser* of the way Moshoeshoe had taken to a westernized life-style:

> Not more than fifteen years ago, he had not as much of a suspicion of the existence of the white nations, and had never seen either a gun or a horse; and at this moment he is perhaps the chief in South Africa who is possessed of the greatest number of horses and firearms. He lives in a capacious and comfortable house, built after the European style, employs five wagons, his own property; and expends annually at least £200 sterling in the purchase of goods of European manufacture. He is now particularly anxious to introduce the cultivation of all European vegetables and fruit trees.

Yet, as this passage unwittingly suggests, Moshoeshoe was highly selective in what he took from European culture. The Kora had shown him the effectiveness of the horse and gun, and he was at great pains to acquire both. He bought large numbers of Colonial horses and a few English thoroughbreds, and in the healthy climate of LeSotho they soon multiplied as a distinct, sure-footed strain known as the 'BaSotho pony'. Guns were more difficult to acquire, and their condition was never good, but by 1852 he could command 'not less than 6,000 well-armed horsemen'. He listened to the missionaries, but was not bound by their advice, and often acted against it. He was careful to dress in European style when entertaining white visitors, but otherwise wore his traditional dress. Though he entertained guests in his European-style house, he preferred to sleep in his own hut. He accepted many teachings of Christianity, even divorcing some of his wives, and abolishing initiation schools, but only in his last days did he contemplate being baptized. He encouraged his followers to listen to the Christian message, but refused to coerce them. Many, indeed, resented his support of the missionaries and were suspicious of their influence on him, believing that they were causing him to abandon Sotho custom. Of course, the missionaries did try to do just that. They were undoubtedly sincere in their sympathy for the BaSotho, but they could not rid themselves of their cultural prejudice against their beliefs. They could find nothing worthwhile in them, and required their converts to give themselves over completely to a European life-style. For that reason, despite Moshoeshoe's patronage, missionary work did not flourish.

Battle for the Land

The missionaries were the tip of a very large iceberg, the vanguard of a juggernaut of European expansion which was rolling steadily towards Moshoeshoe. The original Dutch settlers at the Cape had evolved into a hardy, restless breed who called themselves Afrikaners, but were generally known as Boers, and who were not easily reconciled to the arrival of British authority which followed as one of the consequences of the Napoleonic Wars. Long used to moving their cattle in search of new pastures, they ranged farther and farther beyond the official borders of the Colony in search of new lands and less irksome governments. On the eastern Cape Frontier they had become embroiled with the Xhosa in a series of increasingly brutal wars. The British themselves had begun to encourage immigration in an attempt to secure frontier zones by settling them more densely. Even without the antipathy between the British and the Afrikaners, the Cape could scarcely contain its white population, and in late 1835 it burst open in the movement known as the Great Trek. Thousands of Boers simply packed their possessions into ox-wagons and crossed the borders, intending to place as much distance between themselves and the British as possible. Their main route took them across the Orange, passing through the western fringes

Eugene Casalis, a missionary of the Paris Evangelical Society, one of the first to take up residence in BaSotho territory. He became a firm friend and adviser of Moshoeshoe.

69

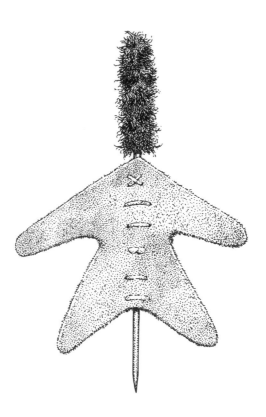

of Moshoeshoe's territory, and on north to the banks of the Vaal and beyond. The Trekkers knew that their interests and those of the African people they encountered along the way were incompatible – both wanted the same land – and their progress was marked by a series of conflicts which broke the power of even the Ndebele and the Zulu.

Moshoeshoe was well aware of the movement, but he adopted a benign attitude. Influenced by the missionaries, he had a high regard for British authority, and he regarded the Trekkers as irresponsible subjects running away from a far wiser ruler. But so long as the Boers did him no harm, he was content to allow them free passage. Gradually, however, as the Trek movement lost momentum, the Afrikaners began to settle the territory between the Orange and the Vaal, and a few adventurous individuals made their way to Thaba Bosiu to beg for farms. Like most southern African peoples, the Sotho did not own land individually – it was considered the property of the nation, though the king had the right to decide who might have the use of it. Moshoeshoe, who was accustomed to allocating tracts on this basis to new adherents, allowed the Boers to graze their cattle on some of his more empty outer reaches, so long as they did not raise any permanent dwellings on it, in the hope that they might provide a buffer between himself and the remaining Kora. He was quite clear that he never gave the land away – it would have been foreign to his outlook to do so. Yet these actions

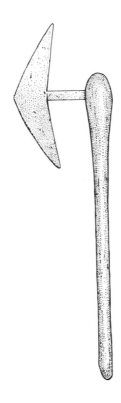

paved the way for the long and bitter wrangles to come, as ever-increasing numbers of whites encroached more and more on the Sotho heartland.

The problem might have been acute enough, but Moshoeshoe's own following was still growing. The *lifaqane* might have stopped, but the BaSotho kingdom still offered the best chance of security and prosperity to those groups who felt isolated or threatened, and wars were still going on elsewhere bringing a steady trickle of refugees seeking protection. Moshoeshoe's only Sotho rival was Sekonyela of the Tlokoa, but he was a less able leader, quarrelsome and constantly at odds with his neighbours, whose cattle raiding tended to drive people away rather than attract adherents. In 1833 Moshoeshoe had had perhaps 25,000 followers; by 1842 it had risen to between 30,000 and 40,000, and by 1865 to 150,000. Sekonyela, by contrast, had about 14,000 followers in 1836, a figure which remained static. In any case the dynamics of Sotho society required constant expansion, since each son of each chief expected to move away from his father's village in time and establish a nucleus of his own supporters. Since the rivalry between heirs was often intense – and Moshoeshoe's sons were no different – it was often impossible for them to live even in the same part of the country. Paradoxically, as Moshoeshoe's reign brought increased stability, the need to cluster together for protection decreased, and the population

Sotho war axe of a style common across the high veld. It was apparently adopted by Moshoeshoe from the Tlokoa.

71

spread, increasing the risk of conflict with rival groups who were also expanding. Moshoeshoe tended to regard his boundaries as all land settled by people who acknowledged his authority, or all traditional lands claimed by them, even if they had migrated. This led to a deterioration of his relationship with Sekonyela, who not only denied some of the BaSotho claims, but found Moshoeshoe's people moving onto his own empty land. A final complication was that a Sotho group called the Rolong had settled on Moshoeshoe's western boundary, with his consent, though they later denied his authority. They were encouraged in this by their resident missionaries, who were Wesleyans, and who refused to place themselves under the influence of the rival French group.

Such a complex situation was bound to lead to friction. Moshoeshoe tried to follow a moderate course, but many BaSotho felt aggrieved, particularly by Boer encroachment, and Moshoeshoe's sons capitalized on this discontent to emerge as the champions of resistance. The Boers, for their part, were making ever-greater inroads into Sotho territory, and were constantly pressing for Moshoeshoe to define his borders in their favour. BaSotho discontent manifested itself in cattle rustling. Tension mounted.

Moshoeshoe's solution was to appeal to the British. He had a great respect for British authority and regarded Queen Victoria as a leading champion of Christian virtues. If the Boers were runaway subjects of the British, then surely the British would be able to curb their excesses and contain them. He, in turn, felt confident he could contain his own followers once they were confronted by the spectre of British military might. For the British, who had recently fought yet another war against the Xhosa, and who had clashed with the Trekkers in Natal, a treaty with a powerful ally across the Orange offered the prospect of shoring up their increasingly battered authority. The governor of the Cape, Sir George Napier, drew up a treaty in October 1843, then sent it on to Thaba Bosiu, where Moshoeshoe added his mark on 13 December.

First Blood

In fact, the Napier Treaty raised as many questions as it answered. It included a vague definition of BaSotho territory which failed to distinguish between Moshoeshoe's land and that claimed by both the Rolong and Sekonyela, thus alienating both groups. British responsibilities were undefined, but Moshoeshoe was supposed to exercise control over all British subjects entering his land. By this, of course, was meant the Boers, and to them the treaty was anathema. They certainly

did not consider themselves British subjects, and they had a profound aversion to being ruled by Africans – as one commandant said in 1843, 'It was written in the Bible that men with white faces and long hair ought never to be governed by a black with crinkly hair'. Their frustration was intense, and they tried to seize the initiative by intimidating one of Moshoeshoe's neighbours, the Griqua leader Adam Kok. But the Griqua had also signed the Napier Treaty, and the British reacted sharply by sending a force across the Orange which dispersed the Boers at Zwartkopjes in April 1843.

Far from improving Moshoeshoe's position, however, this flare-up merely aggravated it. Napier had been succeeded by Sir Peregrin Mait-

The Griqua were of mixed racial origin, and had adopted many aspects of western culture, including horses and guns, which made them formidable marauders in the interior.

73

land, and Maitland's solution was to propose a new treaty. A British resident would be established to keep the peace beyond the Orange, and Moshoeshoe should mark out the portions of his territory in which he was prepared to allow European settlement. Moshoeshoe – who by this stage estimated that there were as many as 300 Boer families living on his lands – agreed to the plan in principle, but the subsequent revised boundary was grossly unfair to the Sotho, confirming most of the Boer claims, and making no attempt to remove those on the Sotho side of the line. The resident, Major Henry Warden, had only a token force to support his authority, and felt he could not risk antagonizing moderate Boer opinion.

Moshoeshoe was patient. He still believed in the integrity of the British, and felt sure the justice of his claims would become apparent in due course. He continued to register protest at Boer encroachments in measured and reasonable terms. He realized that his ally was preoccupied elsewhere – fresh fighting broke out on the eastern Cape in April 1846. He even offered to aid them by supplying warriors to fight the Xhosa, an offer which was politely declined. He felt his loyalty was rewarded when, in December 1847, the new British governor, Sir Harry Smith, crossed the Orange and announced his intention to undertake a thorough review of the situation there.

Sir Harry Smith was a remarkable character, a Peninsular War veteran who served once before on the Cape frontier, and was now returning, covered in laurels, as 'the Hero of Aliwal', fresh from a spectacular victory against the Sikhs in India. Flamboyant and egotistic, he burned with a dynamic energy, and in South Africa he allowed his undoubted eccentricities full flow. He regarded Africans either as children of nature or wilful barbarians, and he lavished sentimental affection and theatrical contempt on them in equal measure. He orchestrated the most extraordinarily melodramatic public displays to impress them with his personality and overawe them with his power. His interview with Moshoeshoe was conducted at typically breathless pace, leaving the king astonished and amused. Yet Moshoeshoe missed a crucial part of Smith's proposals, for, while he proffered the protection Moshoeshoe had long been waiting for, he also baldly stated his intention to annex the whole of the territory between the Orange and the Vaal. On 3 February 1848 it became the Orange River Sovereignty.

Inevitably, Smith's plan caused uproar. The Boers were bitterly opposed to it; they mustered their forces and moved on Warden's residence at Bloemfontein. Since he had only a handful of troops to support him, Warden was forced to retire back across the Orange. In September, however, Smith advanced swiftly from the Cape, met the Boer forces at Boomplaats, and routed them. Warden's authority was re-established, and one of his first acts was to try to establish fixed boundaries for the various peoples under his command. He had chosen

a time of particular turmoil on Moshoeshoe's northern border. Sekonyela, after complaining bitterly of Sotho encroachment, had finally taken matters into his own hands and attacked an ally of Moshoeshoe living on his land. The Sotho had immediately retaliated, to Moshoeshoe's annoyance, and a full Tlokoa/Sotho war seemed inevitable. Sekonyela suggested asking Warden to arbitrate and Moshoeshoe agreed, but negotiations broke down and skirmishing continued. In his attempts to assert his authority, Warden became entangled in a complex web of claim and counterclaim, which involved not only the land itself but also the tally of booty allegedly taken during raid and counter-raid. The wrangles continued throughout 1849 and

Typical Boer at the time of the wars with the Orange Free State in the 1850s and 1860s. The Free State had no standing army, and each Boer provided his own gun and wore civilian clothes. By this time, percussion guns had almost completely replaced the old flintlock models of a generation before.

75

1850 and gradually widened to include the disputes with the Rolong and the Afrikaners. Warden adopted an increasingly harsh line with Moshoeshoe, insisting that he accept stricter and stricter boundaries. Cattle raids and minor punitive expeditions became commonplace. Moshoeshoe tried to restrain his followers, but he was losing faith at last in the British. In December 1850 a new and serious outbreak occurred on the Cape frontier, and this time, far from condemning the Xhosa, Moshoeshoe saw them as fellow Africans making an inevitable stand in the face of intolerable European pressure. He even sent a deputation to the Xhosa prophet Mlanjeni to ask his advice, and, though Moshoeshoe did not follow his instructions to slaughter his herds as a sacrifice to ensure victory, some Sotho did. The British, no doubt nervous at the prospect of a widespread African uprising, reacted harshly in February 1851 and dispersed refugees from the frontier who sought sanctuary in Sotho territory. Then, in May, the dispute with Sekonyela flared up again, and Warden placed the blame on Moshoeshoe's followers. In June he collected a force of 2,500 men, including 161 regular troops, with two six-pounder guns, and 120 farmers, the rest being Africans, mostly Rolong. He marched them north to attack the groups who had been harassing Sekonyela. Feeling among the Sotho was by now running high. Moshoeshoe's sons began gathering their regiments and, reluctantly, the king himself agreed to join them. They intercepted Warden at his camp at Konoyana (Viervoet) on 29 June.

Warden's men were all well armed and he was confident the BaSotho would collapse before his superior firepower, but he had over-estimated his allies and underestimated the determination of the Sotho. The Rolong launched a successful attack on local Sotho living on Konoyana hill, but then dispersed to round up their cattle. The main Sotho forces came up and caught them scattered, inflicting heavy losses. Many Rolong were pinned against the cliff edge and were driven over. At the same time other Sotho launched a furious mounted charge against Warden's camp, and only the presence of the guns prevented them from overwhelming it. Some sources suggest that Warden's losses were over a hundred, while Moshoeshoe lost no more than sixteen men. Morale in Warden's camp collapsed, and the next day his forces made a hasty retreat.

A Dog when Beaten . . .

The disaster at Konoyana had dealt a severe blow to British prestige.

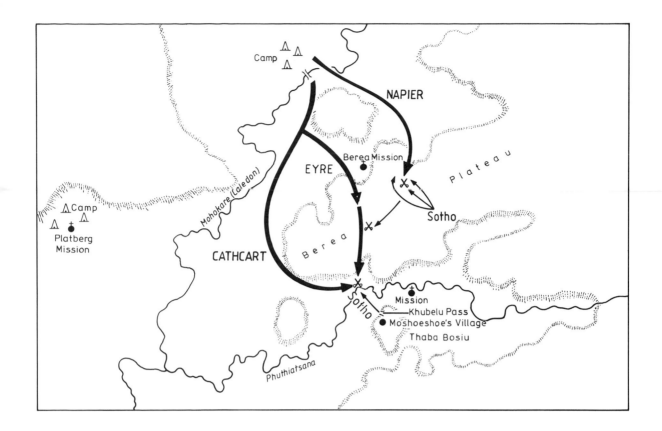

Warden attempted to regroup his forces, but there were few new troops available because of the fighting on the frontier. Moshoeshoe kept a tight grip on his own warriors, refusing to let them continue the attack, while piling on the political pressure by trying to split Warden from his allies. In the end, the war on the frontier discredited Smith's policies so much that he was relieved of office and new commissioners were sent out by the Colonial Office to try to restore order not only there but in the Orange River Sovereignty as well.

The commissioners began their work in early 1852 and concluded that, although the government had made mistakes, the Sotho had re-acted far too violently in their quarrel with Sekonyela. There the matter rested until November, when the new governor, Sir George Cathcart, finished mopping up on the eastern frontier, and rode across the Or-ange at the head of 500 infantry and 2,000 cavalry to meet Moshoeshoe. In fact, the British were fast losing faith in the whole idea of the Sovereignty, which Smith's impetuosity had forced on them, and which was proving both expensive and a failure, but Cathcart was determined to restore Britain's military reputation at all costs. This involved humbling the BaSotho by forcing Moshoeshoe to pay a huge fine in cattle to compensate the alleged victims of his raids. A meeting

The battle of Berea, at which Moshoeshoe defeated Sir George Cathcart on 20 December 1852.

77

British private of the 12th Lancers, in the uniform he would have worn at the battle of the Berea in December 1852: a short dark-blue stable jacket with red facings, and blue trousers with a double red stripe. The 12th seem to have made few concessions to African conditions, beyond wearing a white cover over their forage caps.

between Cathcart and Moshoeshoe took place on 15 December, and was stormy. Moshoeshoe was evasive, and Cathcart lost his temper:

'The time is short, and the cattle are many', said the chief. 'Will you not allow me six days to collect them?'

'You had time given you before . . .'.

'That is true, but I have not now control enough over my people to induce them to comply with this demand, however anxious I may be to do so.'

'If you are not able to collect them', replied the governor, 'then I must go and do it; and if any resistance be made it will then be war, and I shall not be satisfied with ten thousand head, but shall take all I can'.

'Do not talk of war', snapped Moshoeshoe, 'for however anxious I may be to avoid it, you know that a dog when beaten will show its teeth'.

Despite Moshoeshoe's best endeavours, the cattle failed to appear by the deadline, and Cathcart moved to put his threat into operation. He divided his force into three columns, and on the morning of 20 December advanced towards the Berea plateau, which lay between his camp and Thaba Bosiu. His intention was to trap the Sotho in a pincer movement and round up their cattle. Sure enough, one column, consisting of cavalry, succeeded in ascending the plateau and did carry off a large herd. As it tried to retreat, however, the Sotho massed to harass the rearguard, and a party of twenty-five Lancers were cut off, caught against a wall which blocked their retreat, and wiped out. An infantry column supporting them by attacking a different part of the mountain

78

had more success, but retired in the face of fierce mounted charges. Cathcart extricated his men and reformed them in a tight regular formation. Once more the Sotho charged them repeatedly with great determination, but this time the crashing volleys and cannon fire proved too much for them. Nevertheless, at the end of the day Cathcart found himself back in his camp with thirty-eight dead and fifteen wounded and few cattle to show for his pains. The Sotho had also been badly shaken, however, being astonished at the coolness of European professional soldiers (the battle is remembered as *Ntoa ea Masole*, 'the Battle of the Soldiers') and dismayed at the ineffectiveness of their own weapons. Moshoeshoe, fearing a further attack, resorted to a strategy that had served him well in earlier days. The next morning a messenger rode into Cathcart's camp with a note from Moshoeshoe:

YOUR EXCELLENCY, – This day you have fought against my people, and taken much cattle. As the object for which you have come is to have a compensation for Boers, I beg you will be satisfied with what you have taken. I entreat peace from you, – you have shown your power – you have chastised, – let it be enough I pray you; and let me no longer be considered an enemy of the Queen. I will try all I can to keep my people in order in the future.

This was a masterly stroke; it allowed Cathcart to save face and preserve the illusion that he had humbled the BaSotho as he had set out to do. He accepted Moshoeshoe's entreaty and peace was granted.

While the British reconsidered their position, one further longstand-

British private of the 73rd Regiment at the Battle of Berea. The campaigns against the BaSotho and Xhosa in the 1850s saw the first moves away from parade-ground uniforms towards a practical campaign dress for British troops. Apparently the, 73rd fought in scarlet shell-jackets, with either forage caps or locally-procured hats, and brown civilian trousers.

ing conflict was resolved. Throughout early 1853 Sekonyela began raiding Sotho territory once more, but this time Moshoeshoe's patience ran out. He yielded to his sons' clamour for retaliation, and in October he summoned an army of 10,000 warriors and marched on Marabeng and Joalaboholo. Sekonyela was caught unawares and heavily outnumbered, and the Sotho attacked with great courage, forcing their way up on to the summits of the strongholds. The Tlokoa put up a desperate resistance, but were hopelessly disorganized. Sekonyela himself later recalled some of the details of the fight:

The [BaSotho] now got in possession of the difficult points of access and threw stones on my people underneath; and five women and one child were killed at these points. My son David with about twenty men got hemmed in a corner. Their powder failed; the [BaSotho] stormed and killed every man but two, David and Moshepi.

Sekonyela himself fled to the safety of the British residency. Moshoeshoe prevented his warriors from ravaging the defeated Tlokoa, and accepted their surrender, incorporating them into his kingdom. He made repeated overtures to Sekonyela himself, but his old enemy was intractable to the end and refused to be reconciled. He died in a British reserve in 1856.

With the defeat of the Tlokoa, Moshoeshoe was indisputably the most powerful African ruler between the Orange and the Vaal. Yet the political situation was about to change dramatically again. On 8 April 1854 the British formally announced that they were abandoning the Sovereignty. The African groups were to resume control of their own affairs; the Boers were to receive their independence under the name of the Orange Free State. For the Sotho the implication was obvious; now there was no one to check Boer encroachment. Curiously Moshoeshoe, for all his disappointments, clung to the idea that the British would not desert him completely. He told his subjects:

The Queen is sitting on the top of a high mountain, looking down at us, her children, white and black, who are playing below and sometimes quarreling too. She is watching us and trying us. Some day, Queen Victoria will come back among us. On that day I shall rejoice as I rejoice at the rising of the sun.

A Good and Fertile Country

The Boer population of the Orange Free State was scattered and disorganized and apparently taken rather by surprise by its new freedom. It elected a parliament, or Volksraad, and chose its first president, who proved a pleasant surprise to Moshoeshoe. Josias Hoffman was a farmer who knew the king well, had traded with him, had been involved in the building of mission stations and had always been fair and sympa-

Moshoeshoe and his advisers in 1860. From left to right, they are RaTsiu, RaBoroko (seated), Mopeli, RaMatseatsana and Lekhooe.

thetic in his dealings with the Sotho. Hoffman and Moshoeshoe tackled the problem of the disputed border with an attitude of mutual good-will. Yet the problems were almost insurmountable. The successive boundary changes had left many Sotho deeply hostile to the whites, and they expressed their frustration in continued cattle rustling. Moshoeshoe's brother, Posholi, epitomized the view of many Sotho. His stronghold Bolokoe lay in the disputed area, and, as a high-ranking chief with a large following of his own, he chafed under Moshoeshoe's authority, ignored his disapproval, and gleefully harassed the Boers. 'They have taken away my country', he declared, 'and those that have done it must feed me.' Nor was there much support for Hoffman among the Boers, who simply wanted the Sotho driven off farms they considered their own. In February 1855 Hoffman was involved in a scandal involving a barrel of gunpowder he had supplied to Moshoeshoe and compelled to resign. His place was taken by Nicolaas Boshof, whose attitude was hostile. The goodwill and accord Hoffman

81

had fostered with the Sotho collapsed. Tension mounted throughout 1857 as the Free State mustered a number of commandos to punish chiefs living in the border areas whom it considered guilty of cattle rustling. Moshoeshoe tried to keep aloof from local squabbles, but by January 1858 the Boers were adopting an increasingly hard line. They were frustrated by Moshoeshoe's apparent duplicity; while he condemned cattle rustling, he seemed powerless to prevent it. Convinced that they had his tacit support, the Boers delivered what amounted to an ultimatum, demanding that he punish Posholi, remove him from the frontier, and compensate the Free State for his crimes. Moshoeshoe was appalled. 'How is it', he asked, 'that laagers are formed in fields I have lent to the farmers? Do they not know that it is I who have placed them on those places . . .? And today why do they fall upon me with guns, when I had received them in peace?' Yet he could not or would not punish Posholi, and on 19 March 1858 the ultimatum expired and the First BaSotho/Free State War broke out.

The Dogs of War

The Free State had no standing army, and, though its citizens could technically be compelled to fight in defence of their own districts, discipline was negligible. The total white population of the Free State was probably about 12,000, but it was impossible to mobilize more than about 1,500 men at any one time. They were, however, all well armed and, long accustomed to using guns in their everyday lives, for the most part good shots. The Sotho, by contrast, could muster 20,000 warriors, most of whom had horses and guns, but whose weapons were of the poorest quality. The Free State tactics were to invade LeSotho from two points, converging on Thaba Bosiu. Moshoeshoe, however, was content to fall back before them and concentrate his forces for a decisive battle in front of his stronghold. The Boer advance was made in the face of constant skirmishing. On one occasion, on 3 April, at a pass known grimly as 'the Hell', Moshoeshoe's son Letsie trapped and massacred a party of sixteen Boers, but for the most part the wild BaSotho charges were always brought up short by the farmers' accurate shooting. On 6 May the Boers came into sight of Thaba Bosiu and formed a defensive laager. Yet they were reluctant to risk a direct and costly assault on the mountain, and, since the Sotho could not penetrate the laager, the war dissolved into stalemate. In the meantime some parties of Sotho had been slipping behind Boer lines to burn deserted farms and carry off livestock. The Boers began to loose heart and argue among themselves, and a few days later broke up the laager and began

to retreat. President Hoffman sent an embarrassed message suggesting peace, and Moshoeshoe, whose resolve had scarcely been tested, replied in characteristic terms: 'My name is [Moshoeshoe] and my sister is called "Peace". I never liked war in my youth, how could I like it now that I am old?'

Both sides agreed to appeal to the British to arbitrate, and in September the governor, Sir George Grey, presided at a meeting between Free State representatives and the Sotho. The result was yet another new boundary, one to which Moshoeshoe reluctantly agreed, but which, once more, favoured the Free State rather than the Sotho. Moshoeshoe's son Masopha summed up the Sotho reaction:

We rejoiced because Your Excellency caused the dogs of war to be put down, but now when we are hoping you will take care of us, we are to be crushed up against the mountains and squeezed to death.

The Grey award had failed to tackle the fundamental point of conflict. In both LeSotho and the Free State the population was growing, and it was not possible for the two groups to use the same land. As the tide of white expansion swamped other areas of southern Africa, so refugees continued to trickle in to Moshoeshoe's territory. The king, moreover, was growing old, and despairing of a lasting solution. His sons were

A battle between BaSotho and Colonial troops. Although this sketch was made in the Gun War of the 1880s, it reflects a style of fighting which was typical of such encounters: the Sotho, mounted, armed and dressed in a mixture of European and African styles, are unable to close with their enemy, and are pinned down at a distance by his superior fire-power.

increasingly taking matters into their own hands, and most of his subjects no longer had faith in his attempts to placate the whites. Throughout the early 1860s friction continued on both the southwestern borders and in the north, where the Sotho overspill was settling of its own volition. In 1863 both sides agreed to go again to the British for arbitration, but the incumbent governor, Sir Philip Wodehouse, merely reinforced earlier boundaries, demanding that the Sotho abandon large areas that they had already occupied. Both the Free State, under the vigorous President J.H. Brand, and the majority of the Sotho, were prepared to settle the issue by force of arms. Moshoeshoe persuaded his subjects to pull back, in some cases abandoning their crops in the field, but in April 1865 there was an ugly incident when some Sotho returned to retrieve their crops only to find Boers already in the act of harvesting them. One farmer was beaten and two others temporarily detained. Brand demanded compensation and Moshoeshoe could not comply. In June war broke out again.

War of the Cannons' Boom

The fighting in the Second Sotho/Free State War was to be far more destructive than in the First. The population of the Free State had increased, and the commandos were further swollen by volunteers from across white south Africa. They were armed with the latest rifles and with artillery, and they were determined not to repeat the error of 1858. Once more they advanced from several different points along the border. The Sotho retreated to their strongholds, some of them trying to repeat the earlier strategy of raiding behind Boer lines. The fighting was bitter and bloody, but the Boers were not to be put off, and their advance was marked by a swathe of burned villages and ruined crops. On 25 June the first commando arrived at the foot of Thaba Bosiu, and over the next few days it was joined by others. This time a serious attempt was to be made on the king's fortress itself. The first attack took place on 8 August, but it was poorly organized and retreated in confusion. A far more serious attempt took place on 15 August. The Boers bombarded the summit with shells and directed a tenacious assault on the main Khubelu Pass. The pass was protected by three lines of stone walls near the summit, but the Boer plan was to skirmish forward among the jumble of boulders on either side of the pass and enfilade each line in turn, knowing that their shooting was far more deadly than that of the BaSotho. The attack was carried out by the Boer leader Louw Wepener and 600 volunteers, and, pushing forward under a hail of shot, boulders and flung spears, it cleared two lines of wall, but

84

Moshoeshoe photographed in 1860, during the visit of Prince Alfred to South Africa. Although he liked to wear European dress on formal occasions with whites, he preferred traditional dress amongst his own subjects. This is deservedly his most famous portrait, which suggests something of the dignity and humanity which struck so many who met him.

became bogged down before the third. Here many of the Boers began to lose heart and slip away, and when Wepener was shot dead as he tried to move from one boulder to another, the assault collapsed. It had come within yards of victory. With the failure of this attack the Boer strategy lost direction, and resorted instead to an increasingly lax siege of Thaba Bosiu. Yet the Sotho, too, were suffering heavily. Towards the end of August Moshoeshoe brought a huge herd of cattle through the Boer lines and on to the summit. Once there, however, it proved a liability, as it soon outstripped the available pasture, and the cattle began to die of hunger in droves, cluttering up the mountain with their rotting corpses. Moshoeshoe, sensing a repetition of the 1858 stalemate, suggested to Brand that the British once more be invited to intervene, but the president was resolute. The laagers broke up and the siege was lifted, but fighting dragged on as the Boers turned instead to raiding crops, driving the Sotho away piecemeal and annexing their land. Early in 1866 they mounted a renewed offensive, forcing several Sotho chiefs to submit. The Sotho were hungry and weary, and in April Moshoeshoe agreed to a peace proposal which gave away yet more land to the Free State.

Yet this agreement merely led to a lull in hostilities. The Sotho used the time to replenish their crops, and when Boer officials tried to occupy the ceded territory they found the Sotho still in full possession. Moshoeshoe's increasingly frantic overtures to Sir Philip Wodehouse had still produced no acceptable compromise, and on 16 July 1867 Brand called out the commandos once more. Casualties mounted on both sides, more crops and villages were destroyed and cattle raided, and several strongholds fell. Most Sotho still supported the war, and Moshoeshoe was prepared to fight on, but it was increasingly obvious that they could not win. Then, at last, Britain acted. Wodehouse was prepared to go beyond the offer of arbitration and interfere directly, offering the BaSotho British protection. He was keen to bring an end to the potentially damaging war, and saw in this move a means of both securing LeSotho and limiting the expansion of Boer power. Moshoeshoe's faith in his old ally had proved justified after all. His reaction was euphoric:

I have not words enough to tell Your Excellency how exceedingly welcome has been the good news which Your Excellency has favoured me with. The whole of my tribe, all the chiefs of [BaSotholand], and myself more than anyone, we are all glad. We have now before us the prospect of lasting peace . . . I have become old; therefore I am glad that my people should have been allowed to rest and lie under the large folds of the flag of England before I am no more.

President Brand was naturally furious, and there was a final flurry of fighting in early 1868 in which Posholi's fortress was stormed and the chief himself killed. But in February a small force of British troops crossed into LeSotho and Brand, unwilling to risk war with Britain, backed down. LeSotho became a British possession.

Peace

The agreement with the British brought peace for the BaSotho, but at a

price. Inevitably, there was a loss of territory. Wodehouse argued long and hard with the Free State representatives, and at last a new boundary was agreed. It was Moshoeshoe who had to give up land once more, but he seemed resigned to it. 'Take the country', he said, 'and do what you like with it; we are all dead.' The alternative would have been far worse. A British representative arrived to oversee the administration of what remained, and the reigns of power slipped slowly and surely from the king's grasp.

Moshoeshoe did not seem to mind. He had, at least, brought the years of conflict to a close and, if he had sacrificed much, had ensured his people's future security. He was by now an old man, well into his eighties, worn out by the years of responsibility and strife. The coming of the British would usher in a new age, and he knew he would not be part of it. His health began to deteriorate. He seemed suddenly frail, and his mind began to wander. His speeches, never concise at the best

A dramatic, late-Victorian engraving of the Boer assaults on Thaba Bosiu in August 1865. Despite some anachronisms, it nonetheless suggests something of the difficulties faced by the attackers.

of times, became more and more rambling. In early 1868 he moved out of his Sotho hut and into his European one, as it seemed to him more comfortable. In September 1869 he had a collapse and thereafter he took to running his business from his bed. Europeans who visited him were shocked by the squalor and neglect of his surroundings.

His last months were dominated by a contest between the missionaries for his soul. During the worst of the wars with the whites he had lost his profound respect for Christianity and had turned back once more to the spirits of his ancestors. Now, approaching death, the Christian message of salvation comforted him, and both Protestant and Catholic missionaries visited him in a last-ditch attempt to win his conversion. Adele Mabille, who was the daughter of his old friend Casalis, and was married to the Protestant missionary at Thaba Bosiu, described a typical meeting:

I tried to remind him of all God had done for him in sending His faithful missionaries who had not been afraid to tell him the truth even at the risk of angering him and being sent away. Though he was a chief we had not been afraid of telling him that he was a poor lost sinner. Thereupon he began to weep and said again and again, 'Oh my child what you say is true. What must I do? What is holding me back? Pray for me.'

He was reluctant, it seemed, fully to accept Christianity while he was still king, fearing that he would be seen to be abandoning his subjects. At a *pitso* on 18 January 1870, however, he formally announced his intention to hand over the throne to his eldest son in his Great House, Letsie, and he told the missionaries he would accept baptism on 20 March. Yet fate was to cheat them of their prize at the last. His health grew worse, and the date of the ceremony was brought forward to 13 February. Two days before, on the morning of the 11th, he died in his sleep.

The funeral was held the next day, and he was buried not far from his village, on the summit of Thaba Bosiu. A vast crowd of his own subjects attended, and so did the missionaries and representatives from foreign nations, both black and white – a cosmopolitan crowd whose unity in goodwill should perhaps be Moshoeshoe's epitaph.

Moshoeshoe's Legacy

Moshoeshoe had long feared that after his death his sons' jealousies would tear his kingdom apart. The advent of British rule effectively prevented that, though rivalries between them remained a theme of BaSotho politics throughout the rest of the century. There were other tensions, too, the result of Colonial rule. In 1871 BaSotholand had been handed over to be administered by Cape Colony, which attempted to

enforce a disarmament policy. In 1880 the Sotho rose in revolt, and Moshoeshoe's son Masopha and Letsie's son Lerotholi waged such a successful campaign that the Colony had to back down. Britain reassumed direct rule, which it maintained until 1966, when BaSotholand was granted independence. The new rulers honoured Moshoeshoe as their founding father, and called the state Lesotho.

Today Lesotho is impoverished and overcrowded, but that has more to do with its political predicament – it is geographically surrounded by the Republic of South Africa and economically dependent on it – than with Moshoeshoe's legacy. In the modern state of Lesotho the BaSotho kingdom has remained sovereign and intact.

Old and new military styles: Masopha (right), the third son in Moshoeshoe's senior house, a dynamic leader during the Gun War, and his standard bearer. The standard-bearer wears typical Sotho war dress of a style which dates from before the lifaqane, and evidently persisted throughout the nineteenth century, despite the introduction of guns, horses and European cast-off clothing.

The BaSotho Army

BaSotho warrior from the Gun War period of about 1880. By this time, traditional styles of dress were being replaced by European cast-offs, patterned blankets, and a straw hat with a characteristic high crown. Their guns were mostly obsolete flintlock 'Brown Bess' or percussion models.

The Sotho military system was based on the age regiment, though the degree of militarization was far less pronounced than it was in, for example, its Nguni counterpart. When Sotho youths reached the age of eighteen or nineteen, they were called together to undergo circumcision and take part in the ceremonies that initiated them into manhood. This shared experience had a profound effect on them, and circumcision-mates were bound to one another by strong ties of loyalty which lasted throughout their lives. In times of war, these circumcision-guilds fought together, and therefore functioned as loosely organized tactical units. This is similar to the Zulu *amabutho* system, but whereas Shaka and other Nguni war lords strengthened the amabutho and made them the basis of kingly authority, this did not happen among the Sotho. Partly this was due to the attitude of Moshoeshoe himself, whose style of rule was very different to Shaka's, and who did not attempt to create a highly centralized state. Moshoeshoe himself had been initiated into such a guild, the Matlama, and he continued to raise such regiments among his own followers until dissuaded from doing so by the missionaries. He made no attempt to control the followers of chiefs who placed themselves under his protec-

90

An excellent study of a BaSotho warrior. Although taken late in the nineteenth century, it captures the appearance of Moshoeshoe's men at the time of the wars against the British and the Orange Free State. This man is wearing traditional Sotho war costume – a breach-hide and an ostrich feather headress – and carrying a characteristic winged shield. As well as a quiver of assegais, he has a battle-axe at his waist – a weapon apparently adopted from the Tlokoa – and carrying a European musket. The Sotho were quick to adapt to horses, causing the British to liken them to African Cossacks.

tion, and allowed them to raise their own regiments. There appears to have been no rigid organization or discipline within Sotho regiments, which were usually led by men of royal blood from within their own ranks. Since Sotho society had an inherent tension between rival chiefs and between the generations – each son seeking to establish a following independent of his father – there was a risk that the military system might exaggerate this. Indeed, Moshoeshoe's inability to control the actions of his subordinates is a perennial theme of BaSotho history, and his enemies were sometimes able to exploit these internal divisions.

Nevertheless, what is striking about the BaSotho army is its consistent success, even when fighting European enemies armed with superior weapons. Unlike the Nguni, whose tactic of massed charges in the open played into their opponents' hands, the Sotho preferred to mount lightning raids or to retire to defensive strongholds. Raiding was, of course, the primary military activity in the days before the lifaqane, and was conducted as stealthily as possible, making the most of natural cover. In the wars against the Free State, Sotho raids behind Boer lines, striking at undefended farms, quickly undermined the morale of commandos at the front. In defence, the Sotho fell back on mountain retreats whose natural inaccessibility was compounded by stone breastworks. At both Viervoet and Berea Sotho forces used cattle as decoys, and attacked when their enemies broke ranks, trapping them against natural obstacles and stone walls.

Sotho regiments did not wear ornate uniforms like the Nguni. Standard male dress was a knotted breach-hide and perhaps a cloak of hide pinned on the right shoulder. In times of war, men wore a dense mop of black ostrich feathers over the forehead. Only men of distinction were entitled to wear leopard-skins, which seem to have been worn around the shoulders, with the arms thrust through holes at the sides. They also wore a curious V-shaped gorget of flattened brass, which hung from a thong around the neck, protecting the throat and upper chest. As contacts with Europeans increased, so changes became apparent in styles of dress. By the 1870s trade blankets were commonly worn, together with a characteristic hat, made of straw and with a high crown, which had apparently been modelled on European wide-brimmed hats.

Sotho weapons were influenced by outside contacts, too. Originally warriors carried a small hide shield, with distinctive projecting wings. This was fastened to a stick at the back, which in the case of important men stuck out two or three feet at the top, and was decorated with black ostrich feathers. This served as a standard and rallying point in battle. Such shields were intended only to deflect light throwing spears, and were no match in hand-to-hand combat for the larger, stronger Nguni spears. Each warrior carried several throwing spears, which were kept in a leather quiver over his shoulder, and perhaps a wooden club. By the 1840s Moshoeshoe had adopted the Tlokoa war-axe, which had a half-moon blade on a tang, which was sunk into a wooden handle.

The BaSotho also adopted both horses and guns in large quantities. They first acquired horses from white traders and, while the lifiqane wars were fought entirely by infantry, the proportion of Sotho troops riding horses steadily increased, so that by the 1880s they were predominantly cavalry. Guns, too, were easily bought from traders, or earned through work at the diamond mines or elsewhere, though they were usually of obsolete pattern, and the Sotho had the greatest diffi-

Chief Lerotholi, the eldest son of Letsie, who was Moshoeshoe's eldest son in his senior house. Lerotholi was another successful BaSotho leader in the Gun War. He is wearing a costume typical of the later Wars, consisting of a patterned blanket, and a high-crowned straw hat, said to have been copied from Boer styles.

92

culty in obtaining spare parts and ammunition – as did most Africans. As a result, eye-witness accounts stress the volume of Sotho fire, but not its accuracy. On one occasion, in 1865, 2,000 BaSotho horsemen charged to within a hundred yards of a Boer commando and loosed a tremdendous volley, which hit only one horse.

Such statistics do the BaSotho a disservice, however, for it should be remembered that their commanders were often quick to adapt to new challenges, and their warriors were skilful and daring. Neither Ndebele, Briton, nor Boer managed to capture Moshoeshoe's stronghold at Thaba Bosiu during his lifetime, and his successors were able to defy the full weight of the Cape Colony during the Gun War, when peace came through negotiation rather than by defeat. There can be no greater testament to the BaSotho's courage and ability than that.

Bibliography

Casalis, E. *The Basutos*, 1861.

King, W.R. *Campaigning in Kaffirland, or Scenes and Adventures in the KaffirWar of* 1851–2, 1853.

Lagden, G. *The Basutos*, 2 vols; 1909.

Omer-Cooper, J.D. *The Zulu Aftermath*, 1966.

Sanders, P. *Moshoeshoe, Chief of the Sotho*, 1975.

Thompson, L. *Survival in Two Worlds: Moshoeshoe of Lesotho, 1786–1870*, 1975.

Tylden, G. *The Rise of the Basuto*, 1950.

Chronology

1786	Moshoeshoe born.
1810	Moshoeshoe's first marriage, establishing his independent status.
1820	Moshoeshoe builds a homestead on Botha-Bothe mountain.
1822	JANUARY? Hlubi and Ngwane clans cross Drakensberg and attack Tlokoa; start of the *lifaqane*.
1823	Matiwane defeats Hlubi.
1824	Moshoeshoe moves to Thaba Bosiu.
1825	First clashes with Kora bands.
1828	FEBRUARY Matiwane attacks Thaba Bosiu and is repulsed.
1831	Ndebele attack Thaba Bosiu.
1833	JUNE French missionaries arrive at Thaba Bosiu.
1835	Beginning of Great Trek.
1843	DECEMBER First Treaty with British.
1848	FEBRUARY Sir Harry Smith establishes Orange River Sovereignty.
1851	30 JUNE Battle of Viervoet.
1852	20 DECEMBER Battle of Berea.
1853	Moshoeshoe finally defeats Tlokoa of Sekonyela.
1854	APRIL Orange River Sovereignty dissolved; withdrawal of British authority and establishment of Orange Free State.
1858	MARCH to SEPTEMBER First War between the BaSotho and Free State.
1865–68	Second War against the Free State.
1868	British intervention brings a halt to hostilities; British authority extended over BaSotho.
1870	11 FEBRUARY Moshoeshoe dies.

Mzilikazi ka Mashobane, the founder of the Ndebele kingdom, sketched by the traveller, William Cornwallis Harris, in 1835. Although curiously stylised, this is the only detailed portrait of the king, and confirms written descriptions of his soft features, and strong, if fleshy, physique.

Mzilikazi
OF THE MATABELE

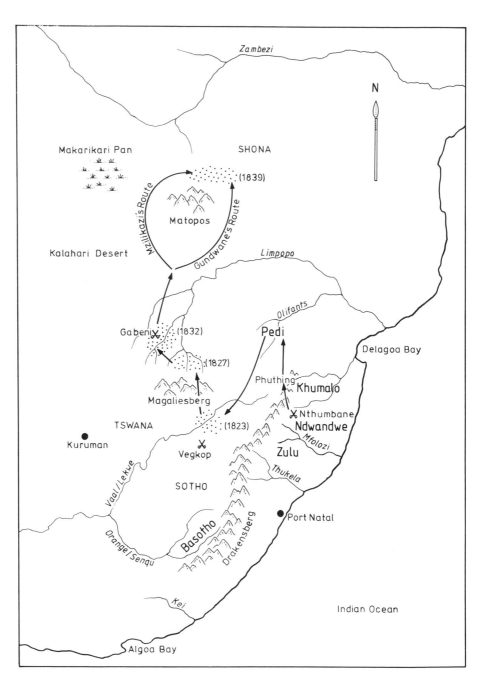

Mzilikazi's migrant Ndebele kingdom in the period 1821–39, indicating periods of settlement with approximate dates of arrival.

Messengers, take these words to [Shaka]: 'Mzilikazi has no king. In peace he will meet [Shaka] as a brother, and in war he will find him an enemy whom he cannot and will not despise'.

(Mzilikazi, to Shaka's envoys)

There he sat – how changed – the vigorous, active and nimble monarch of the Matabele, now aged . . . he drew his mantle over [his] face [for] it would have been an awful sight to see the hero of a hundred battles wipe from his eye a falling tear.

(Robert Moffat, on Mzilikazi's decline)

The Great Road

Mzilikazi of the Ndebele – the Matabele – was an able and ruthless general who carved out his own nation by conquering and incorporating those around him. He was forced out of his homelands by the Zulu but, with remarkable resilience and tenacity, struggled to rebuild his authority in a series of alien environments. Each time he was driven on by natural hardship or war, surviving the ravages of various African and white enemies, until he finally came to rest north of the Limpopo River, hundreds of miles from his birthplace. Mzilikazi was certainly not the only black leader to adopt a migratory life-style, and indeed, such wanderings were a typical response to the upheavals of the time. Mpangazitha of the Hlubi, Matiwane of the Ngwane and Soshangana and Zwagendaba of the Ndwandwe were all renowned marauders who tried to establish themselves in foreign lands. Yet Mzilikazi was the most successful of them all. The Ndebele kingdom, in its final form, was the wealthiest and most powerful of these states, incorporating a wide variety of people from different cultural backgrounds and infusing them with a sense of common nationhood. It derived many of these attributes from the personal qualities of Mzilikazi himself. That his kingdom survived his death in 1868 and the succession crisis that followed it, and was only broken thirty years later in two brutal wars against Europeans, is proof of his success. Although the monarchy was overthrown, that sense of nationhood was not displaced, and the Ndebele who still live in the Matabeleland district of modern Zimbabwe consider themselves the inheritors of a proud tradition.

As far as the literate outside world was concerned, Mzilikazi and his people burst out of the wilderness and faded back into obscurity several times. For years they were known only by rumour and half-truths, and, until permanent contacts were finally established, there were long gaps between their encounters with the wandering explorers, hunters, traders or missionaries who were their only link with the European world. As a result, European descriptions of Mzilikazi himself, recorded years apart, are not always consistent. Robert Moffat, a missionary who was perhaps his closest white friend, thought he was short, as did fellow missionary Andrew Smith. The traveller, Captain W. Cornwalis Harris, however, thought he was tall. All agreed, though, that his physique was muscular, despite a tendency to fat, and that he had a round face and a pleasant smile. His voice was light and effeminate, and his moods variable, though he was generally pleasant and amiable, concealing his thoughts behind a cultivated façade of shyness. Only his piercing eyes gave away his true nature. In fact, his strength of character was remarkable. Although his father had been only a minor chief, Mzilikazi believed unquestionably in his destiny to rule. He was haunted by the insecurity of his days in Zululand and the fear of Shaka's wrath, but the unknown held no terrors for him, and he tackled it like every other challenge, with confidence and vigour. He was a charismatic leader, and a bold but flexible military commander. Like most of his contemporaries, he was ruthless in the maintenance of his power, but he was also a pragmatist – he knew that, unlike Shaka, he could ill afford to use terror as a political tool, dependent on a small band of followers and surrounded by enemies as he was. As a consequence, he was more liked by his subjects than were Shaka or Dingane, and his passing was regarded as a genuine national tragedy. Most of all, of course, Mzilikazi was a survivor.

Son of Mashobane

Mzilikazi, whose name, appropriately, means 'The Great Road', was born sometime in the 1790s. His father was Mashobane, chief of a subsection of the Khumalo clan, and his mother was Nompethu, who was related to the royal house of the Ndwandwe chief Zwide. The great upheaval of the *mfecane*, when Shaka's marauding warriors wrought devastation, was scarcely under way, but even at this early stage Zwide was a powerful and wealthy man. Mashobane's Khumalo lived in what is now northern Zululand, along the banks of the Insikwebesi River, only a few miles west of Zwide's territory, and they probably acknowledged their powerful neighbour as their overlord. It has even been suggested that Mzilikazi grew up amongst the Ndwandwe. In any case, Mashobane's people were too closely associated with the Ndwandwe to avoid being drawn into the conflict that was disturbing the region.

Zwide was involved in a power struggle, trying to extend the influence of the Ndwandwe, and until about 1816 his main rival was the Mthethwa chief Dingiswayo. In that year, however, Dingiswayo

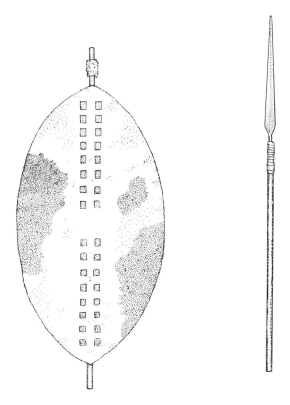

helped his protégé Shaka secure the throne of the Zulu, and Shaka's rapid rise soon eclipsed his patron. Zwide triumphed over Dingiswayo – he apparently lured him into a trap and murdered him – but when he tried to do the same to Shaka, Shaka was warned by a friend amongst the Khumalo. Zwide was furious with his allies for betraying him, and attacked them and killed Chief Mashobane. In his place he set Mzilikazi on the Khumalo throne. This was a fairly common response to the problem of disloyal subordinates – both Dingiswayo and Shaka were known to have secured control over lesser clans by installing their own clients as chiefs. Mzilikazi, however, clearly felt no love for Zwide, for as soon as an opportunity presented itself he deserted him and went over to the enemy.

This took place against the background of two major Zulu/Ndwandwe wars. In 1818 Zwide sent his army against Shaka but was defeated at Gqokli Hill. In 1819 he reorganized his forces and tried again, but this time Shaka retreated before his advance, adopting a scorched-earth policy. When the Ndwandwe were hungry and demoralized, Shaka attacked them at the Mhlatuze River. The Ndwandwe were scattered and Zwide was driven north, where he eventually died. Mzilikazi played a small but significant role in this. All the evidence suggests that he was a loyal supporter of Zwide during the

In the early days of Mzilikazi's kingdom, these Ndebele weapons reflected their 'Zulu' origins, though they gradually changed to assume a style of their own. War-shields became shorter, with the stripe of hide, which bound on the stick, less tightly laced. Stabbing spears were often smaller and less well made than the Zulu prototypes, and a number of other spear types were adopted from peoples encountered by the Ndebele during their travels.

1818 campaign, but that he switched sides in time to be on the winning side during the second war. One can only speculate on his motives, but Mzilikazi could scarcely have trusted Zwide, after his treatment of the Khumalo, and he was far too astute to tie himself too closely to a loser.

His reward was to be accepted into the Zulu state as an ally. There has been much discussion amongst historians as to his exact relationship with Shaka, some suggesting that Mzilikazi became a close personal friend of the Zulu king and achieved high rank within the Zulu kingdom. This is probably based on a misunderstanding of Shaka's position at this time. Shaka had only just emerged as a major figure in the *mfecane* struggle. He had been stunningly successful, but his kingdom was by no means as highly centralized as it later became. Many of its component parts had joined him as allies rather than by conquest, and Shaka allowed them considerable autonomy under their own chiefs, provided they acknowledged his overall authority. The fact that Mzilikazi remained in command of a regiment drawn from the Khumalo suggests that he enjoyed exactly this sort of relationship. It does not, however, imply that he had resigned himself to Zulu rule. His later career proved that he was no man's vassal, and he probably joined Shaka as a temporary measure, to free himself of Zwide and to avoid the taint of defeat. Within a year or two, as Shaka consolidated his power, Mzilikazi began to find Zulu authority irksome.

Defying Shaka

The circumstances of his rift with Shaka are well known. Around 1820, Mzilikazi led a raid on a Sotho chief to the north and returned with a large herd of looted cattle. As Shaka's subject, he was required to hand most of this booty over to the Zulu state. It would have been absorbed into the royal herds and redistributed throughout the kingdom, and much of it would probably have been given into Mzilikazi's keeping. This was a subtle balance of obligation and reward, but Mzilikazi chose to deliberately flout it. He sent Shaka a derisory offering – as few as four cows, according to some traditions. Shaka naturally sent his envoys to investigate the matter. What happened next is captured in a dramatic account supposedly based on eye-witness testimony. Mzilikazi shouted to his own warriors:

'Surround these dogs, and cut the tops from their plumes.'

Slowly and without a word we hemmed them in, but not a hand was raised to touch those marks of royalty. Mzilikazi saw our hesitation, and red now grew his eyes with passion, and pressing his way through his people, with his own hands he plucked the crests from off their

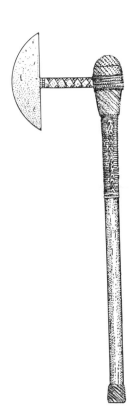

heads, and seizing a battle-axe, he laid them down one by one across a block and hacked them through. When done he handed back the stumps and each in silence took it. . . .

Then spoke Mzilikazi: 'Messengers, take these words to [Shaka]. Show to him the stumps of the plumes and say that Mzilikazi, son of [Mashobane] thus addresses him. Mzilikazi has no king. In peace he will meet [Shaka] as a brother, and in war he will find in him an enemy whom he cannot and will not despise. . . . Depart! and tell your king it rests with him whether it be peace or war.'

Presumably, Mzilikazi hoped that he could simply throw off Shaka, and rule as a independent chief, but Shaka could hardly afford to let him. At first, the king sent a small punitive force, which attacked the Khumalo somewhere on the Insikwebesi River. Mzilikazi beat it off, and then retired north to a stronghold on the Nthumbane hill. Shaka sent a fresh force, and this time the fighting was fierce and the Khumalo were scattered. Many of their women and children were killed, and all their cattle rounded up. Mzilikazi himself escaped with about three hundred of his followers, mostly warriors. Now he had no choice but flight, and as he did so he fell on a chief named Nyoka, who lived on the Mkuze, about a day's march to the north. Taken by surprise, Nyoka was driven out, and Mzilikazi remained in his lands just long enough to gather up his cattle and crops. Then he crossed the barrier of the Drakensberg west of the Usutu River and pushed on into the interior. It was the beginning of an epic journey.

The knobkerry remained a standard weapon across southern Africa, whilst the axe with it's half-moon blade and heavy wire decoration, is typically Shona.

Strangers from the East

The Sotho people of the interior had already begun to suffer from the overspill of the horrors of the mfecane. The Hlubi of Mpangazitha and the Ngwane of Matiwane had erupted over the mountains some time before, and were ravaging the country to the south. Ripples of disruption from their conquests had passed through the Transvaal shortly before Mzilikazi burst upon the scene, crowding the Sotho groups north and west. Mzilikazi, too, would find that the sophisticated military techniques of the coastal belt, the large shield and short stabbing spear with which his warriors were armed, would give them a huge advantage over the poorly organized and lightly armed Sotho. The Khumalo might have been few in numbers, but they were an ideal raiding force, lean and hungry veterans with few possessions or non-combatant passengers. Their first victims were the Phuthing Sotho, who were routed with typical ease, and driven away to the west. Mzilikazi then headed north, and attacked the Ndzundza people of Chief Magodongo, and his ally, Chief Sibindi. The Ndzundzu were originally an Nguni group who had crossed the mountains generations before and settled among the Sotho, and they seem to have retained some of the Nguni military flair, for this was a battle of unusual tactics:

Their impis joined, and came out to give us battle, driving before them a large herd of white cattle, so that they might conceal themselves amidst the dust it raised.

This mode of warfare was known to us by its wide repute, and the king, discerning the purpose for which they came, sent ahead a posse clattering their shields, which frightened back the cattle to their owners. In the stampede we charged them home, inflicting serious loss. We then marched on to the kraals, which we found deserted. Of cattle, sheep, and goats, however, there were plenty and we took them unto ourselves. The grain, too, in much abundance was taken to supply our wants.

This account captures the essence of Mzilikazi's policy on his arrival in the Transvaal – attack, drive out the local inhabitants, seize their foodstuffs for his own people, then move on. Yet there is evidence that Mzilikazi was looking for a more secure and permanent base, even at this early stage. There are a number of traditions which suggest that he established a homestead about this time, which he called *ekuPumuleni*, 'the Place of Rest'. But the Ndzundza territory proved a far from ideal place to settle. It was suffering from drought, and it was still within striking distance of Shaka's Zulu. After perhaps no more than a year, Mzilikazi moved north again, this time into the territory of the Pedi.

The Pedi would emerge later in the nineteenth century as one of the most powerful Sotho-speaking groups of the interior, but when Mzilikazi encountered them they were weakened by internal dissension. A Pedi chief named Thulare had begun a process of expansion, but Thulare had died, and his sons were squabbling between themselves when Mzilikazi swept through their land in 1822. Disunited, they fell

easy prey to the invaders. When Mzilikazi's warriors caught the Pedi royal family, only one man escaped alive, a son of Thulare named Sekwati who later rebuilt the Pedi kingdom. Yet Pediland was clearly not the refuge Mzilikazi was seeking, for once again he stayed just long enough to strip the country bare of livestock and grain.

This time he ventured south to the middle reaches of the Vaal (Lekwe) River. This was occupied by a Sotho group, the Khudu, but they were easily dispersed. It is interesting to pause to consider the fate of the Sotho. Ever since Mzilikazi's followers had burst over the Drakensberg, they had been dislodging Sotho groups, most of whom fled north and west, creating a regional wave of the *lifaqane* (the Sotho version of the word *mfecane*) which was causing so much devastation further south. Cut off from their food supplies, a vast mob of starving refugees drifted across the high veld attacking any more settled communities in their path. By the middle of 1823 they were threatening Dithakong, the capital of the Tlhaping people. This was the site of the London Missionary Society's Kuruman mission station, run by Robert Moffat. Moffat, determined to defend his hosts, appealed to the Griqua and Kora for help. These two groups were descended from the original Khoi inhabitants of the Cape, a mixed race who had interbred with both black and white. They had adopted many aspects of European

Warrior of the Pedi, one of the high-veld peoples whom Mzilikazi encountered early in his career of conquest. Their appearance was similar to that of most of the high-veld Sotho and Tswana groups.

culture – notably guns and horses – but, accepted by neither society, they lived in a cultural half-world on the frontier of European settlement. Moffat secured the aid of scarcely a hundred Griqua, and on 26 June 1823 they confronted the Sotho horde, which numbered thousands. In a running fight which lasted seven hours, Sotho numbers proved no match for Griqua mobility and firepower. After losing about five hundred dead, the Sotho horde broke up. The survivors fled, and many later attached themselves to stronger marauders operating in the vicinity. Ironically, some even joined Mzilikazi, the architect of their woes.

Mzilikazi stayed on the Vaal for five years. He frequently sent his army on raiding expeditions, and they returned laden with booty. Yet even here Mzilikazi did not feel safe. The Griqua success at Dithakong had convinced them that they were a match for any Africal group, and from 1825 they combined in temporary alliances with local Sotho chiefs and made a number of raids on Mzilikazi's outlying cattle outposts. Mzilikazi naturally retaliated, but he was no more able than the Sotho to defeat them in an open fight. In the middle of 1827, he gathered up his followers and moved north. They crossed the Magaliesberg mountains and descended into the basin of the Oori River. As with their previous migrations, the Sotho already occupying this territory were able to mount no concerted opposition. Some submitted to Mzilikazi, while others simply abandoned their homes and fled.

The Ndebele

The northern slopes of the Magaliesberg were to be Mzilikazi's home between 1827 and 1832. No doubt with the mountains at his back he felt more secure, though he always took the precaution of creating a depopulated no-man's-land around his settlements. As he explained to a visiting hunter:

all his warfare was purely defensive. To that end he conquered and exterminated . . . he excused his wholesale massacres in the Transvaal as an act of policy. 'I was like a blind man feeling my way with a stick. We had heard tales of great impis that suddenly popped up from underground or swept down on you from high mountains . . . and we had a dread of the Korannas, mounted and armed with rifles. I had to keep open veld around me. Had I been attacked every one of them would have been a spy and a recruit for my enemies'

It was in the Transvaal that Mzilikazi's people ceased to be mere marauders and began to assume a new nationhood. The Sotho made few distinctions between the rampaging bands from the coastal belt, and, as Moffat recorded, simply reported that they 'have been driven from

their country by a tribe they call Matabele'. There is much discussion as to the precise meaning of the term *Matabele*. It has been translated, rather romantically, as 'those who disappear behind long shields', but it seems to have been a blanket name refering to 'strangers from the east'. Nguni groups who crossed the Drakensberg generations before were called Matabele, and so, it seems, were Matiwane and Mthimkhulu's followers in the south. Yet in Mzilikazi's case the word has stuck, and his people are universally known either as Matabele, or by their own version of the same word, *Ndebele*. It took many years for this word to become widely adopted, however, and throughout Mzilikazi's lifetime they referred to themselves by terms that reflected their coastal origins – Khumalos, Nguni, or even Zulus.

During this period, the nation also underwent a change in its cultural make-up. Mzilikazi had escaped, it will be remembered, with scarcely three hundred of his own people. Constant military activity would have whittled that down long before it could be replaced by natural reproduction, so it was necessary to expand by incorporating outsiders.

Fellow Nguni, who were not only considered inherently superior, but who were better fighting material, were prized recruits. Mzilikazi's following grew with a steady trickle of dissidents and refugees from Shaka's wars, but he also reaped a rich reward from the continuing clashes between rival Nguni war lords on the high veld. In 1825, the long-standing contest between Matiwane and the Hlubi was resolved in an epic battle which smashed the Hlubi. A Hlubi survivor, Madubangwe, describes how he was captured wandering in the veld by the Ndebele, and gradually incorporated into the nation:

I was one of a party which wandered far after Matiwane scattered us . . . [and the Ndebele] captured us. One raised his spear and said 'Let us kill the jackals.' But the leader said: 'No, we want boys to help us in driving the cattle.' They gave us food, and we followed them [to Mzilikazi's homestead].

[Mzilikazi] loved to see dancing, so I was kept at the 'great place'. After a time I was given a spear and a shield. Then I got a wife – a woman captured from the Bangwaketse.

In 1826, there was another major conflict which produced a stream of refugees, some of whom joined Mzilikazi. The Ndwandwe of his old overlord, Zwide, now led by Zwide's son, Sikhunyana, moved down from the eastern Transvaal, where they had fled after the disastrous battle of Mhlatuze in 1819, and tried to take back their old lands from Shaka. Shaka intercepted them in the northern Drakensberg foothills, and smashed them once and for all. The survivors scattered, and some of them reached the Ndebele.

Despite these windfalls, however, it was impossible to keep the Ndebele a nation of pure Nguni. As early as the Pedi campaign, Mzilikazi's regiments had brought away human captives as well as cattle, and during the Transvaal period large numbers of Sotho were absorbed. Many were individual captives, who were simply grafted on as a lower social class and given menial tasks. Others were entire chiefdoms which submitted to Mzilikazi's authority and were allowed to remain largely intact so long as they gave tribute. Sketches by white travellers in the 1830s show Ndebele warriors wearing Zulu-style costume and carrying typical oval shields and stabbing spears, though many individual warriors must by then have been Sotho in origin, and some vassal chiefdoms supplied their own contingents for Mzilikazi's campaigns. The Nguni age-regiment remained the basis of the military system, and physically Mzilikazi arranged his kingdom to give plenty of warning of an enemy's approach, with outlying, lightly populated cattle posts on his borders and denser settlements nearer his own base. Administratively, he ruled like all coastal Nguni kings. His authority was dictatorial, but he was advised by a close inner circle of councillors, the *Mpakathi*, and a wider gathering of chiefs from within the nation, the *ibandla*. The ibandla functioned as a limited mouthpiece for ordinary Ndebele, an outlet for public opinion that provided a curb on tyrannical excesses. Inhabiting an oasis in a desert of so many enemies,

Mzilikazi could ill afford to alienate his own people.

The nation depended on its army to survive. It is very unlikely that an average Ndebele army of this time numbered more than a thousand warriors, although larger forces could be mustered in time of dire emergency. Ndebele military success was based upon superior weapons and tactics rather than numbers, and they were more than a match for the local Sotho, upon whom they continued to prey regularly. In 1831 Mzilikazi launched the army against the southern Sotho, but it was unable to dislodge either Sekonyela or Moshoeshoe from their mountain strongholds. On the whole, however, the Ndebele must have felt that the northern slopes of the Magaliesberg had at last offered them a secure base. Yet even here there was danger.

The Griqua

Mzilikazi's success as a cattle raider had attracted the attention of the Griqua and Kora during his previous sojourn on the Vaal. By the end of the 1820s, his herds must have reached epic proportions, and the Griqua began to cast covetous eyes across the Magaliesberg. In 1828 the Griqua leader Jan Bloem forged an alliance with the chief of the Taung Sotho, Molitsane, with the intention of creaming off some of Mzilikazi's cattle. In July their combined forces, several hundred Griqua and several thousand Taung, crossed the Magaliesberg passes. If Mzilikazi had been counting on the mountains to provide him with advance warning of enemy approach, he was to be disappointed. The Griqua fell on the nearest cattle posts with very little opposition, since the main Ndebele army was away raiding elsewhere. They shot down the herdsmen, rounded up their cattle, and retreated back across the mountains. Molitsane took his share of the spoils and returned to his own territory as quickly as possible, but the easy victory had made the Griqua over-confident. An Ndebele woman taken captive tried to warn them about the danger of a counterattack, but the Griqua scoffed at her. Haip, a Griqua survivor of the expedition tells what happened next:

The third night arrived without any direct evidence of danger. The party proceeded to slaughter and feast upon part of the cattle they had secured and in that congenial occupation they passed the greater part of the night . . . they betook themselves to rest just as the moon was descending below the horizon . . .

With the appearance of morning, the prophecy of the woman was to be fulfilled. When the approaching day could just be discerned and the revellers were buried in sleep, the [Ndebele] rushed to the charge, and, as would be expected . . . flight rather than defence was immediately resorted to by the attacked.

In the confusion a few shots were fired, but . . . perhaps more the result of inadvertency than of any regular aim. Haip, accompanied by a bushman, effected his escape from the camp; and shortly afterwards, when daylight was fairly established, he discovered that not only himself, but many of the [Sotho], were within a circle of [Ndebele] warriors placed from six to ten yards apart, and ready to destroy whoever might be found flying.

Haip himself slipped through a gap when the warriors were distracted by other escapers, but the Ndebele tactics were clearly very successful. They recaptured almost all of their lost cattle, and had killed over half the Griqua. Nevertheless, Mzilikazi was not content with this retribution. He waited the best part of a year, then prepared his army for a major attack on Molitsane, the Griqua ally. This force, consisting not only of Nguni but of his Sotho vassals, is said to have numbered 4,000 men, an extraordinary size given the Ndebele population at the time. Molitsane had little hope of standing against it, and he abandoned his capital and retreated south, but the Ndebele caught up with him on the Modder River, and smashed him. Hundreds of Taung were killed, and all their cattle taken. Molitsane himself escaped and after various adventures found refuge with the BaSotho leader Moshoeshoe.

Meeting the White Men

In this clash with the Griqua and their allies, Mzilikazi had won a major triumph. It was not the last, but before battle was rejoined an event took place which was to hold great significance for the future. In the years since they had first settled on the Vaal, the Ndebele had gradually come to the attention of wandering white traders, hunters and missionaries. In return, Mzilikazi was only too aware of the power of Europeans. In July 1829 a chance meeting between an Ndebele patrol and two white hunters led Mzilikazi to issue an invitation to the missionary Moffat to visit him. Mzilikazi had heard of the part played by Moffat at the battle of Dithakong, which had invested him with enormous prestige. The message reached Moffat at Kuruman, and he dutifully set out on a long wagon-trek to the Ndebele capital. His first meeting with the king was short, but it sowed the seeds for a lifelong friendship between them. Mzilikazi, of course, had no real need for spiritual enlightenment – like many of his contemporaries, he saw the missionaries as vital diplomatic links with the world of the whites and as a means by which he might gain access to such European goods as guns, powder and horses. In due course, he would allow missionaries to preach in Ndebeleland, but this was of little consequence compared to the communications channel that Moffat's station at Kuruman represented. Moffat has left us a splendid description of the full panoply of

Mzilikazi's court at this time. The king organized a magnificent dance in Moffat's honour:

Some thousand warriors had collected on a smooth plain outside the town. The warriors were formed into a kind of circle, about three or four men deep. A number of war songs and national airs were sung, and one of these was composed for the occasion. Sometimes [Mzilikazi] took his stand in the centre, with a shield of lion skin, and a well-polished common butcher's knife, which he had from me, in one hand, and which seemed to please him very much, as its bright surface reflected the rays of the sun. He appeared to be chief musician, while all looked towards him and punctually imitated every motion he made in accordance with the music. To some of the tunes they danced manfully while he looked on with apparent indescribable pleasure. The appearance of his men in full dress was much like the dress of a regiment of Highlanders, colour excepted. A great number of strings or strips of skin, with the fur twisted, hung like a kilt around the middle, reaching to the knees. Similar tails adorn the arms and neck, while the head is decorated with a profusion of feathers. In the centre of the forehead a long blue feather stands, like a cockade. Each regiment has its own peculiar mode of adorning the head, as well as the

Robert Moffat, the Scottish missionary who worked amongst the Tswana for nearly fifty years, and who formed a remarkable life-long friendship with Mzilikazi.

colour of the shields. All the [amadoda], or married men, have a piece of otter skin, stuffed like a roll, tied around their foreheads. This is also worn by [Mzilikazi] himself. On this occasion he had, instead of tails, small bunches of beads of different colours, suspended from his middle, while from each shoulder he had about fifteen pounds of beads (like two thick ropes), crossing over the breast and reaching to the feet. He evidently felt their weight and not infrequently leaned upon [my] shoulder or arm. His head was adorned with the finest feathers, formed into a couple of small bunches. His countenance exhibited much self-complacency while the air echoed with his praises, his achievements, his power and his greatness, with the most extravagant epithets, such as King of the Heavens, King of Kings, etc, etc.

Mzilikazi's desire to make an ally of the whites was heightened by his further troubles with the Griqua. Throughout the 1830s the Griqua chief Barend Barends tried to raise support for another attack on the Ndebele. Barends claimed lofty motives – to free the Sotho from Mzilikazi's harassment – but, like Bloem before him, he had his eye on the Ndebele herds. By July 1831 he had mustered three hundred Griqua horsemen and hundreds more Sotho allies. The resulting campaign was a grim replay of the first expedition. Once again the Ndebele regiments were away, raiding far to the north, beyond the Limpopo, when the Griqua attacked and once again the invading force easily rounded up the Ndebele cattle. Learning nothing from their previous experience, however, they were just as slack in their security arrangements on the return journey. One night they herded the cattle on to a ridge, then went to sleep in small encampments surrounding it without troubling to appoint sentries. The Ndebele struck before dawn. Many Griqua were killed as they slept, others shot each other in the confusion, and many were trampled by the cattle. The defeat was even more comprehensive than in 1828; most of the Griqua were killed, and the Ndebele recovered their cattle. The battle dispelled the Ndebele dread of firearms, and the warriors marked their victory by killing captured horses and piling guns into a heap and setting fire to them.

Mzilikazi was content. Once again he had outgeneralled the Griqua, and they were rapidly losing any terror for him. Even guns seemed to him to be of limited usefulness, since his warriors could overwhelm them before they could be reloaded. Yet this second Griqua campaign had also highlighted a number of weaknesses in the Ndebele defences. In particular, the Magaliesberg had proved no barrier against attack, and Mzilikazi began to make plans for another migration. He was given a sharp push by the sudden and dramatic re-appearance of his old enemies, the Zulus.

Dingane Strikes

For most of his career, Mzilikazi had lived in dread of an attack by

Shaka. This had never transpired, because Shaka had been too involved in his own conquests to worry about the continued defiance of a distant upstart. But in 1828 Shaka had fallen victim to a palace coup and been murdered by his brothers, one of whom, Dingane, succeeded him on the throne. Dingane lacked Shaka's aggressive mentality, but in order to consolidate his internal power it soon became necessary for him to mount a successful military campaign. No doubt he was looking for a suitable candidate when news of the Griqua raid on Mzilikazi reached him. Presumably reasoning that the Ndebele were likely to be weakened by such an experience, he despatched a large force under the command of Ndlela kaSompisi in July 1832. It covered the 300 miles to Mzilikazi's territory in under a month, and caught the Ndebele by surprise. The Zulus sacked several outlying settlements and carried off a herd of cattle, but the Ndebele rallied and counterattacked. An Ndebele informant described something of the fighting:

We found them at the 'Ndinaneni kraal, and fought them there; but as they had the protection of the huts, behind which they took their cover, we were first vanquished and then chased. Behind a bush we rallied, and as our pursuers came sharply round a bend, thinking that we were still flying on before, we fell upon them, and so great was their surprise, though they numbered ten to our one, we drove them back with heavy loss, and turned the tide against them.

113

In fact, the fighting seems to have been costly but indecisive, and the Zulus retreated, hurrying away what captured cattle they could.

It was enough for Mzilikazi. In August he organized a series of raids on Sotho settlements along the Marico river, a hundred miles to the west, and, shortly after, his people abandoned the Magaliesberg and migrated.

The Marico Valley

In all likelihood, Mzilikazi intended to settle permanently in the Marico valley. The country itself was congenial, it was farther from the Zulu and, an added bonus, it was closer to the main routes through the interior used by the whites. Moffat's mission station at Kuruman lay only 350 miles southwest of Mzilikazi's new capital, Gabeni. The king was very keen to establish permanent contacts with Europeans, whom he regarded as potential allies. Increasingly, he used Moffat as a door-keeper to his kingdom. Mzilikazi remained highly suspicious of anyone approaching his kingdom from the southeast – the direction from which the Zulus and Griqua attacks had come – but anyone who approached him through Moffat, and sent word of his coming, was welcome. A steady trickle of whites wandered Ndebele territory hunting and trading. In 1835 Moffat secured permission for a scientific party from the Cape, led by Dr Andrew Smith, to visit Mzilikazi's court. Moffat himself accompanied the party, which ensured them a delighted reception. Smith was allowed to explore the country north of the Marico, and on his return he suggested that Mzilikazi should send a diplomatic mission back with him to the Cape. Mzilikazi eagerly accepted, and two Ndebele officials made the long trek south to the Colony. They were entertained for six weeks in Cape Town, where every attempt was made to impress them with the power and sophistication of European culture. Their reward was a treaty signed by Governor Benjamin D'Urban himself, in which the British and the Ndebele nation pledged – rather vaguely – to deal with one another in a friendly manner, and Mzilikazi agreed to accept resident missionaries.

Meanwhile, the Ndebele settled into their familiar way of life in the Marico valley. By now a large proportion of the population was Sotho-speaking, but Mzilikazi continued to raise and train new regiments in the Nguni way. Visitors were struck by the fact that Sotho communities continued to exist unmolested right in the heart of the kingdom, though of course their inhabitants were regarded as menials by the Ndebele. Military activity continued, but without the urgency of previous years; most of Mzilikazi's neighbours had already accepted the

umcwala

Young warrior of the Matabili — the feathers indicates that he has already shown bravery in battle — and he ranks as a proved soldier & as an A.B. (and so on) & an able bodied fighting man

inevitable and bowed to his authority. In May 1834 the Griqua tried to mount a fresh raid, but, astonishingly, fell into exactly the same trap as on the previous expeditions. They swept down on undefended outposts, rounded up the cattle and retired. Three days later the Ndebele caught up with them and routed them.

This third clash between the Griqua and the Ndebele was significant more for its unfortunate repercussions than for its own sake. Mzilikazi was furious that the Griqua could still presume to attack him, and Ndebele sensitivity to unwarranted intrusion was honed to a fine edge. In August 1836 parties of men with wagons, riding horses and carrying guns, ventured across the Vaal in the south. They were strangers who had not alerted Mzilikazi to their presence. The king immediately mustered a small force and sent it to investigate. It came across a

Another sketch by Baines, who visited the Ndebele kingdom in Zimbabwe shortly after Mzilikazi's death, showing a warrior in full ceremonial regalia. At that time, the old Zulu style of dress was dying away, in favour of a distinctive Ndebele fashion. This man wears a headring, marking him out as a married warrior, and a Zulu-style headband, but his headdress and cape of black ostrich feathers is typically late Ndebele.

number of undefended camps, attacked them, and wiped out the inhabitants. The wagons and guns were taken to Gabeni in triumph.

But the victims had not been Griqua, as the Ndebele probably supposed. They had been whites, the vanguard of the Boer migration known as the Great Trek, and the consequences of this attack would prove calamitous for the Ndebele.

The Voortrekkers

The Boers, or Afrikaners, were descendants of the first Dutch settlers at the Cape, who over the centuries had developed into a tough, independent-minded and self-reliant breed of frontier farmers. Used to living off the land, most were good horsemen and good shots, and many had grown accustomed to wandering, driving their herds beyond the borders of the Colony each year in search of fresh pasture. In their outlook they had much in common with black Africans, and instinctively understood that, as pasturalists, they were both in competition for the same resource, land. Yet most held the Africans in contempt; deeply religious, they were convinced that God had intended them to play a dominant role on the African continent. Nor were they very fond of the British, whom the twists and turns of political fortune during the Napoleonic Wars in Europe had established as the new rulers of the Cape. By the 1830s many Afrikaner families were so disenchanted with the British administration that they were prepared to pack their possessions into their ox-wagons, and simply move off beyond the Colony's borders and into the interior. This was the Great Trek, an exodus of white settlers comparable to the black mfecane. It began in 1835 and lasted for the best part of a decade. It was not a united movement, since its leaders constantly quarrelled among themselves and their followers often changed allegiance or struck out on their own. Nor did it have any precise objectives, beyond the search for a 'promised land' where the farms were empty and limitless, the cattle thrived, and there were no British officials to interfere. There was, of course, very little land in southern Africa that was not already claimed by somebody, but as the Trekkers advanced through those areas unsettled and depopulated by the lifaqane, their hopes were fulfilled. The party attacked by Mzilikazi in August 1836 had been members of the Erasmus, Botha, Steyn and Liebenberg families. They had been camped along the Vaal while their leader, Hendrik Potgieter, reconnoitred ahead, and, failing to observe etiquette by asking Mzilikazi's permission, had crossed into Ndebele territory to while away the time by hunting. One or two of the camps had had a few

moments warning of the Ndebele attack and had been able to drive them off, but in the rest as many as fifty whites had been killed.

The clash seems to have taken both sides by surprise. Potgieter hurried to the scene and decided to pull back his straggling party to a more secure defensive position on the Renoster River. Not strong enough to press forward, unwilling to retreat further, they waited to see what Mzilikazi would do next. By now Mzilikazi must have been aware of their true identity, but he refused to allow access to his kingdom through any route other than by Kuruman. In October he gathered an impi, placed it under the command of his most trusted military commander, Kaliphi, and launched it to the attack.

The Boer position was a strong one, drawn up below a low ridge later christened *Vechtkop*, 'Fight Hill'. Potgieter's forces numbered only thirty-five adult men, with a number of women and children, but they had drawn fifty wagons into a defensive circle, or *laager*. Each wagon was lashed to its neighbour, and the gaps between them were filled with thornbush. An inner shelter, protected by ox-hides to stop flung spears, had been built to house the children and wounded. The women had been kept busy casting lead balls and sewing them in little bags to serve as buck-shot. The only disadvantage was that there was no room to

Boer Voortrekker in the typical costume of the 1830s. The Trekkers favoured short jackets, and carried their powderhorns attached to their waist-belts. Their ideal weapon was a heavy double-barrelled hunting gun called a roer*, which sometimes had hide sewn around the fore-stock to protect the hands when the barrel over-heated.*

contain the party's livestock, which, in the event of an attack, would simply have to be abandoned.

The Ndebele forces arrived on 15 October, having covered the 175 miles from Gabeni in a week. Potgieter and his men rode out to meet them. Potgieter called out to them urging them to parley, but, according to one account, an Ndebele spokesman shouted back 'Mzilikaze alone issues commands, we are his servants, we do his behests, we are not here to discuss or argue, we are here to kill you!' Another source, however, suggests that the attempt to negotiate had scarcely begun when a nervous Boer fired into the Ndebele ranks. In any event, the Ndebele rose up with a shout and charged forward. The Boers, being mounted, were too quick for them, and a running fight developed as Potgieter galloped back to the laager. A wagon was rolled aside to let them in, and the Boers rushed to their posts around the barricade.

The battle of Vechtkop remains a decisive chapter in the long and bloody history of racial conflict in southern Africa in the nineteenth century. It proved once and for all that even a small party of skilled and determined men, armed with horses and guns, could hold off any number of spear-armed infantry. Kaliphi's warriors encircled the wagons and squatted down out of rifle range while their commanders considered their next move. This lull went on for several hours, and the tension within the laager must have been unbearable. Then the Boers heard a stream of shouted commands and the Ndebele rose up, formed into two groups, and charged down upon the laager on either side, drumming their spears against their shields as they did so. At thirty yards' range the Trekkers opened fire, and their hail of shot cut great swathes through the ranks. The warriors vaulted their dead and hurled themselves against the wagons, shaking and rattling them in their attempt to find a way in. One Boer woman saw a black hand groping towards her from the far side of the barricade, and she seized an axe and lopped it off. For several minutes the Ndebele stalled while the Boers poured fire into them at point-blank range. Then they pulled back to regroup. Changing tactics, they came on again, this time pausing to throw their spears high over the wagons and into the centre of the laager. Over a thousand spears were gathered up after the fight, to the Trekkers' astonishment, but their effect was negligible. With the failure of this second attempt, the Ndebele withdrew. To console themselves they rounded up the Trekkers' enormous herd of 6,000 cattle and 40,000 sheep.

In fact, the battle had been something of a stalemate. The Ndebele had lost perhaps five hundred men altogether, and they had failed to destroy the Boers. Only two Trekkers were killed, but the loss of their livestock was a tremendous blow, since without their oxen they could not move. They had to await the arrival of fresh Trek parties and friendly Africans before they could even dismantle the laager.

Catastrophe

Neither Potgieter nor Mzilikazi can have thought that Vechtkop was politically decisive, yet when the Boers returned to the attack they seem to have taken the Ndebele by surprise. It is a curious fact of Ndebele history that, despite their dread of surprise attacks, they so often fell victim to them. Potgieter, reinforced by Gert Maritz and his followers, raised a commando of about a hundred mounted men, and secured the help of a large body of Sotho. In January 1837 they set out to regain their livestock and to teach Mzilikazi a lesson. This time they skirted west, and approached the Ndebele from the direction of Kuruman, whence attack was least expected. Their targets were the most southerly Ndebele settlements in the Mosega valley. Their approach went completely undetected and early on the morning of 16 January they struck. An American missionary who had recently arrived in the country vividly described the attack:

Afrikaner men and women manning the defences at the battle of Vechtkop, 16th October, 1836. Having blundered into a war against the Voortrekkers, Mzilikazi was unable to over-run their laagers. But the Boers were immobilised by the loss of their cattle, and the battle was effectively a stalemate.

119

Sometime before sunrise, we were aroused by the startling cry, 'A commando! A commando!' In half a minute . . . a brisk fire commenced on a kraal of people a few hundred yards from our house. The fire of one followed that of another in quick succession . . . in a few minutes we were in the midst of a slaughter. The people fled towards our house. . . . Those who fled were pursued by the Boers with a determination to avenge themselves for the injury they had received. . . . Several balls passed over our house, some struck it, and one passed through Brother Venable's chamber window. . . . . The Boers attacked and destroyed thirteen, some say fifteen, kraals. Few of the men belonging to them escaped, and many of the women were either shot down or killed with assegais.

We have no means of ascertaining how many lives were destroyed. We suppose from two to four hundred.

The raid was a complete success, and the Boers rode home with about 6,000 head of cattle. They had lost only two of their African allies. The missionaries, fearing for their safety, decided to abandon their stations and left with them.

The survivors of the attack fled Mosega and streamed north towards Gabeni. Mzilikazi must have been shocked and appalled by this unexpected disaster, since he made no attempt to pursue the Boers, as he had the Griqua. Before he had time to recover, the Zulus dealt him a fresh blow. King Dingane – whose intelligence system was obviously better than Mzilikazi's – soon heard of his rival's misfortune and decided that it was an appropriate moment to renew their long-standing feud. He despatched an army which marched swiftly and secretly inland, searching first for the Ndebele in their old haunts on the Magaliesberg, then advancing towards Mosega. From here they followed the signs of flight to Gabeni. The Zulus seem to have been seriously weakened by the rigours of the march, however, and the resulting battle was again stiff but inconclusive. Nevertheless, the Zulus did manage to escape with a large number of Mzilikazi's cattle.

Coming on top of the Boer foray, the Zulu attack was very serious. The Ndebele were demoralized and impoverished, and Mzilikazi had been made only too aware of his continued vulnerability. He reacted as he had always done before, and began to make plans to move the entire nation north. But the worst was yet to come.

Retribution

The Boers considered their attack on Mosega to be a temporary punishment for Mzilikazi's crimes against them. They planned to return as soon as possible to settle the score with him once and for all. Internal squabbling prevented an immediate start, but in October 1837 Potgie-

ter, with all the tenacity of an avenging angel, allied himself with a newcomer, Pieter Uys, and mustered a force of 360 Trekkers, supported again by a number of Africans. By the beginning of November they had reached the Mosega basin, and, like the Zulus, followed the signs of flight, which led them towards the Ndebele. On 4 November they struck the first settlements. Once again, they had caught the Ndebele by surprise. The Trekkers gunned the warriors down as they tried to form up. Driving a mob of refugees before them, the Boers pressed on, attacking one important settlement after another in a running fight said to have lasted nine days. At one point the Ndebele tried to form up in their traditional 'chest and horns' encircling movement, but Potgieter directed his men to concentrate their fire on the tips of the horns, and the line buckled and disintegrated. So many bodies were strewn about the site of this incident that the Boers named a distinctive hill which overlooked it *Maaierskop*, 'maggot hill'. On the morning of 9 November, the commando advanced on Gabeni itself. Mzilikazi was determined to make a stand here, and some accounts suggest that he directed his battle in person. The story has it that, as the Ndzundza had once tried to over-run him by stampeding their cattle towards his warriors, so Mzilikazi drove his great herds towards the Boers, but their firing turned them back on the Ndebele. Whether this was the case, or

This bas-relief frieze at the Voortrekker Monument, Pretoria, portrays the final battle between the Boers and the Ndebele in the Transvaal, at Gabeni, as an epic struggle of man and beast.

121

whether there was simply a confused mêlée as Mzilikazi tried to extricate his herds, cannot be known for sure, but the result was the same. The Ndebele regiments were broken and the Boers chased them from the field. They harried them for days, rounding up enormous numbers of cattle, and setting fire to every village they came across. By the time Potgieter called a halt, the Marico valley was a scene of utter desolation. The Boers were masters of all they surveyed, and Mzilikazi and the Ndebele were fugitives once more.

Exodus

At the height of Mzilikazi's power in the Transvaal, in about 1834, his followers, it has been estimated, numbered about 20,000. They had been depleted by a series of epidemics and wars, but perhaps 15,000 people followed the king as he moved north to escape the carnage. This time there was no planned migration preceded by military attack. The retreat was a shambles, a disorderly stream of individuals or small bands, driving whatever livestock they had managed to salvage, who gradually came together with other parties, until they crossed the Limpopo in several long, straggling columns. Fortunately for them, the owners of the lands into which they were now trespassing had already suffered from Ndebele raids, and were not inclined to resist. For a while it must have seemed as if the whole nation was disintegrating. Many Sotho-speakers, who had not long been incorporated, took advantage of the confusion and rugged country to slip away.

Behind them, the Ndebele left a power vacuum which was to sow the seed of future tension in the Transvaal. Many of the Sotho groups who had supported the Voortrekkers had done so in the hope of regaining land stolen by Mzilikazi. Yet the expulsion of the Ndebele provided the Trekkers with just the excuse they were seeking to legitimize their own territorial ambitions. They seized the entire Transvaal by right of conquest, and refused to acknowledge that the Sotho had prior claims. In fact there were not enough Boers to populate the area, and the empty Ndebele territory gradually filled up with both Afrikaners and Africans, living in uneasy coexistence.

Ndebele ijaha, *or young warrior, in the costume of the 1890s. The headress and cape of ostrich feathers are characteristic of the appearance of the Ndebele in their days in Zimbabwe.*

The subsequent wandering of the Ndebele has passed into legend. Beyond the Limpopo, in Ngwato territory, they paused long enough to regroup, and celebrated by performing the *inxwala* ceremony, an annual reaffirmation of nationhood usually associated with the new harvest. Then, having devastated the Ngwato grain-stores and crops, they moved on. For several years the Ndebele were beyond the reach of

white observers, so we know little of Mzilikazi's thinking. For some reason never satisfactorily explained, he divided his followers into two roughly equal groups. Command of one was given to an induna remembered as Gundwane Ndiweni (perhaps another name for Kaliphi), while the king led the other. Gundwane's party included a number of the king's wives and sons, including Prince Nkulumane, the heir apparent, so presumably the separation was not intended to be permanent. Gundwane's party moved eastwards for a while, parrallel to the Limpopo, then turned north. Mzilikazi headed west into the arid veld of modern Botswana. It is impossible to say if either party knew where they were going – there had been some limited Ndebele penetration beyond the Limpopo, which Kaliphi may have commanded. Gundwane's division certainly marched with a sense of purpose; it finally came to rest in the Matopos hills of modern Zimbabwe in the middle of 1838.

Mzilikazi's party, meanwhile, wandered in the wilderness. They went northeast until they struck the Makarikari salt pan, where they halted for a while. The area was sparsely populated, but there were sufficient inhabitants for Mzilikazi to replenish his food stocks by raiding them. Then they turned east, following the Nata river. With hindsight, and no contemporary evidence to shed light on the matter, the journey seems aimless, but Mzilikazi was probably exploring local rumours in an attempt to find a new home that would meet his security requirements. At one point he seems to have considered crossing the Zambesi, but as he approached it, he ran into tsetse-fly country, as his friend Moffat later described:

He with his company and a great many cattle had no sooner entered the tsetse region when scores died. He instantly saw that advance without them, and of course without food, would be impossible, when he commenced a retreat in direct course to where he now lives. From their ignorance of the locality of the tsetse, it was some days before they got out from among them. The cattle died so rapidly that their carcasses were lying within sight of each other along the course they had taken, and where they halted for the night, hundreds were left dead.

By this time, he had been out of contact with Gundwane's party for months, and had no idea where they were. As he drifted east, however, towards the Matopos, Mzilikazi encountered a local hunter, who told him of Gundwane's settlements and offered to lead him there. About the middle of 1839, the two parties were reunited once more. But for the king himself it was scarcely a happy reunion.

Hill of the Indunas

For some time, Gundwane's party had been plagued by rumours that

Two young Ndebele warriors in the 1890s, wearing ceremonial regalia, and carrying a typical selection of weapons.

the king had been massacred by a hostile tribe, or had perished in a desert wasteland. The annual inxwala ceremony was due to be performed early in the year, and Gundwane must have been nervous about postponing this enormously important religious festival. After the trauma of defeat, the nation needed to be reassured. Yet the king's role in the ceremony was crucial. He embodied the unity of the nation and their link with the ancestral spirits and, without him to perform certain rites, no one would be free to gather the new harvest. There was, however, no guarantee that Mzilikazi would ever return and, after much agonizing, Gundwane decided to install the heir, young Nkulumane, as king, and to proceed with the inxwala.

Mzilikazi arrived while the preparations were in progress, and was appalled. It seemed to him that he had been betrayed by the very people he had relied upon to protect his interests. It was tantamount to rebellion, and he responded with typical ruthlessness. Gundwane and all the chiefs who had supported him were executed. A long, flat-topped hill marks the spot, and is still known as *Thabayezinduna* 'the hill of the indunas'. The fate of his heir, Nkulumane, remains a mystery. It was illegal to shed the blood of royalty, so some say he was tied to a tree and strangled, but rumours persisted for years afterwards that he had really been sent into exile, or had escaped. Mzilikazi's next senior son, Lobengula, only survived because an induna hid him until the king's wrath passed.

Matabeleland

In their new lands north of the Limpopo, the Ndebele had at last found a home, and they were not to move again. They spread out across southwestern Zimbabwe, a district universally known as Matabeleland. The original inhabitants, the Shona-speaking Kalanga people, were in no mood to resist. Until recently they had been part of an extensive empire called the Rozvi, but this had been devastated almost a decade before by other Nguni bands fleeing Shaka's wars. Mzilikazi established his settlements north of the Matopos without opposition. Later European accounts made much of lurid stories of his treatment of the Shona, but his cruelties were greatly exaggerated, and in fact he treated them much as he had done the Sotho in the Transvaal. Some fled to inaccessible hilltop sanctuaries, while many were incorporated into the Ndebele kingdom. Others became allies and some merely paid tribute. Once the first wave of conquest was over, military activity against them was limited, and was aimed at punishing resisters. Later in the century, the Ndebele would claim authority over most of the Shona in eastern

Zimbabwe, but their control away from the centres of royal authority was very limited. Like the Sotho, the Shona also made their contribution to Ndebele culture. They believed in a God called *Molimo*, who spoke through the mouths of priests at various sacred caves and hill sites around the country. Far from rooting out and destroying this alien sect, Mzilikazi treated it with respect, and it gradually came to be accepted into Ndebele belief.

Ndebele society had always been class-based, and during the more stable years in Zimbabwe the class system solidified. The original Nguni element, Mzilikazi's Khumalo and those refugees from Zululand who joined him later, formed the top layer, known as *Zansi*, 'those from down-stream'. The Sotho and their descendants, who had been considered menials in the Transvaal, were now elevated to a middle

Lurid Victorian sketch depicting an Ndebele raid on the Shona in Zimbabwe. Such sketches were used as propaganda by the British South Africa Company to justify its war against Mzilikazi's successor, Lobengula. Although the Ndebele did raid the Shona, interaction between the two groups was more complex than such deliberate images suggest.

class, the *Enhla*, 'those from along the way'. Shona speakers now filled the role of underdogs, and were known as *Holi*, apparently a term of contempt. An Ndebele informant has described how social relations functioned between the three groups:

A Zansi male could take an Enhla woman to wife to propagate our species, yet seldom did an Enhla male take to wife a Zansi woman, but when he did both were treated with contempt as having done a thing they never should have done . . . and as the Enhla women grew less by reason of their marriage with the Zansi, the Enhlas did here and there take Holi women to wife. . . . The offspring of a Zansi male and Enhla woman took the *isibongo* [family name] of his father. . . . The only ones of pure race that have so remained down to today are just a few family of [indunas] that intermarried their untainted bloods. With these one little drop of outside blood prevented a union.

In Zimbabwe, too, the Ndebele political system reached its logical conclusion. It remained modelled on its Zulu origins, but adapted to the nation's particular circumstances. At its centre was Mzilikazi himself, who organized new settlements, planned military expeditions and judged his people's legal cases. Like many black southern African rulers, he has been portrayed in the past as a despot, and there can be no doubt that Ndebele law had frequent recourse to the death penalty. Yet Mzilikazi was not by nature cruel, and he seldom had so many subjects that he could afford to massacre them wholesale. In his foreign policy he was concerned to control the Shona, and the 1840s brought a short-lived but menacing reappearance of the Boers. The years following the expulsion of the Ndebele from the Transvaal saw dramatic swings in Voortrekker fortunes, and profound rifts in their leadership. By 1845 Mzilikazi's old enemy Hendrik Potgieter, disenchanted with his colleagues, was once more ranging far and wide in search of new territory. When he discovered the location of Mzilikazi's kingdom in 1847 he crossed the Limpopo with a band of two hundred horsemen and a number of African allies, intent once more on stealing the king's cattle. There was some slight skirmishing, in which Potgieter's Africans suffered heavily, and he withdrew. His appearance naturally alarmed Mzilikazi, but in fact the Boers lacked the will to undertake another major war against the Ndebele. In 1852 Potgieter's representatives visited Mzilikazi's court and opened negotiations, which finally brought peace between them.

The Mountain Falls

During the early 1850s, Mzilikazi made several attempts to find out what had happened to his old friend, the missionary Robert Moffat.

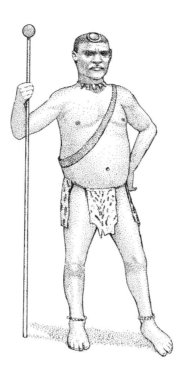

Much has been written about their relationship, most of it based on Moffat's own journals, which inevitably present a one-sided picture. The king's desire to find his old friend probably had a lot to do with his need for a trusted go-between, now that Europeans had found his whereabouts again. Yet, for all that, the two men seemed genuinely fond of each other. Moffat was still at Kuruman, and in 1854 a messenger reached him from Mzilikazi, and once more he set out on a long and arduous journey to meet him. The King received him at his Mahlokohloko homestead on 17 July. Mzilikazi was delighted to see him, but Moffat was shocked at the deterioration in the king's appearance. He was probably not yet sixty, but:

King Lobengula, Mzilikazi's son and successor, who presided over the downfall of the Ndebele kingdom.

There he sat – how changed! – the vigorous, active and nimble monarch of the Matabele, now aged, sitting on a skin, with feet lame, unable to walk or stand. I entered, when he grasped my hand, gave an earnest look, drew his mantle over [his] face. It would have been an awful sight to see the hero of a hundred battles wipe from his eye a falling tear.

The exact nature of Mzilikazi's illness has not been determined, though Moffat, noticing that he quaffed huge quantities of beer, primly blamed it on intemperance. He may indeed have been suffering from cirrhosis of the liver. Certainly, neither the small supply of medicine Moffat brought with him, nor anything his own healers could provide, brought much lasting relief. The decline in his health was commented on by many of the whites who visited him over the next few years, who diagnosed it variously as gout or dropsy. In 1860 he was described as an 'old half-naked porpoise of a human being', and in 1863 as 'a physical wreck. His lower limbs are paralysed'. He was 'a frail, palsied old man, in his second childhood, unable to move a yard'. Many of his subjects felt he was bewitched, but frequent 'smelling out' ceremonies seeking the evildoer failed to secure his recovery. Whatever the cause, he was a shadow of his former self, and his illness brought with it a return of his old fears. He remained haunted by the possibility of a Zulu attack, though he was now far beyond their strategic reach.

The king's last years were marked by a steady increase in traffic among the whites. Hunters, traders and prospectors all made their way to him, having first been cleared by Moffat. Ominously, one of them, Henry Hartley, discovered gold in a disused Shona mine in 1865. Mzilikazi remained well disposed towards them, and even allowed missionaries to take up residence in his country, at Inyati, though their labour fell on stony ground. Since he could rely on Moffat once more, the king had no use for their diplomatic services, and neither he nor his subjects were in the slightest bit interested in Christianity.

In 1868 the king's health collapsed completely. For several months he lay at death's door, beyond the reach of Ndebele healers, then, on the afternoon of 5 September, surrounded by his councillors, Mzilikazi kaMashobane, the Great Bull Elephant of the Ndebele, the father of the nation, died. For a month his death was kept a closely guarded secret, while his wives kept watch over his body, which remained wrapped in blankets in his hut, and the indunas made preparations for the transition of power to his heir. Then Mzilikazi's death was announced, and the nation was summoned to the capital. Mzilikazi's body was placed in a wagon, along with his possessions, and, accompanied by the regiments in full panoply, it was taken to the Matopos. The procession halted at the foot of a hill named Nthumbane, and the corpse was carried up the slopes and laid in a granite cave. Then the wagon was dismantled and, together with its contents, placed in a second cave. Both were sealed with stone walls. The procession made its way back to the capital, and cattle were sacrificed to the king's spirit.

Mzilikazi's journeys were at last at an end. His history had been extraordinary. He had witnessed the rise of the great Shaka, defied him, and survived. He had seen the coming of the Boers, and survived them, too. He had conquered, lost almost everything, then conquered again, and his legacy was his nation. The Ndebele mourned him: '*Intaba seyidilike* – The Mountain has fallen'.

The Fly and the Chameleon

Mzilikazi's death created a political crisis within the Ndebele state. His

senior surviving son, Prince Lobengula, was his obvious successor, but some elements within the kingdom refused to accept his claim. Some even believed that Nkulumane was still alive, waiting for the call to ascend his rightful throne, though all attempts to find him ended in failure. In the end, the Zwagendaba ibutho openly refused to support Lobengula, and a brief but bloody civil war ensued. Lobengula mustered his own forces, and attacked and destroyed Zwagendaba's principal settlements.

It was Lobengula's misfortune to rule his people at a time of vigorous European expansion. The trickle of visitors to his father's homestead became a flood of importuning adventurers, seeking permission to hunt elephants or prospect for gold. Throughout the 1870s and 1880s, the European grip on southern Africa tightened, and rivalry between the Boer and British states intensified with the discovery of gold and diamonds. Lobengula came under severe pressure to allow the commercial exploitation of the country north of the Limpopo. Caught between the innate conservatism of his people, who resented white interference in their affairs, and the military threat posed by the Europeans, Lobengula is said to have likened himself to a fly, waiting unhappily on a branch for the tongue of the stalking chameleon to strike. In 1890 he was persuaded by the diamond magnate Cecil Rhodes to allow the British South Africa Company to occupy the Shona territory in eastern Zim-

Ndebele warrior of the Imbizo regiment in 1893, at the time of the war with Rhodes. By this time, the Ndebele army had adopted a uniform style of dress, with headresses and capes of black ostrich-feathers. Only the colour of the shields and additional plumes in the headress served to distinguish the regiments. The Imbizo were King Lobengula's senior élite regiment.

babwe. The so-called Pioneer Column trekked across the Limpopo, skirted the main Ndebele settlements, and established a base at Fort Salisbury.

It was Rhodes' intention to exploit the whole of Matabeleland, which he hoped might contain gold to rival that found in the Transvaal. In 1893 he provoked a war with Lobengula, and two columns armed with machine-guns invaded Matabeleland. Lobengula sent his regiments to oppose them, but in two sharp fights they were heavily defeated. Lobengula fled, and Rhodes became master of both Matabeleland and Mashonaland, a country he named Rhodesia. Lobengula died a broken man, a fugitive on the banks of the Zambesi.

Yet Rhodes' private-enterprise occupation of Matabeleland was not the success he hoped, since the tales of gold proved largely unfounded. European settlement was badly organized, and failed to grasp that the Ndebele had not been thoroughly suppressed. Many areas had been untouched by the fighting in 1893. In 1896, conservative Ndebele elements seeking to restore the royal family allied with priests of the Molimo religion to organize a rebellion. Outlying white farms and mines were attacked, and for several months the settlers were forced to take refuge in a laager in Bulawayo, a town built by Rhodes on the ashes of Lobengula's capital. The rebellion later spread to Shona-speakers independent of Ndebele influence. Both risings were eventu-

Trooper of Cecil Rhodes' British South Africa Company forces, who finally overthrew the Ndebele kingdom in 1893. The Company's men were all volunteers, who were issued minimal military clothing, and who mostly fought in civilian dress. They were armed with the Martini-Henry rifle.

ally defeated, but only after heavy fighting. The Ndebele won some concessions to their grievances, but the royal family was not restored, and all traces of the military system were broken up.

Today the Ndebele live in the independent state of Zimbabwe. Mzilikazi is revered as a hero among them, and his grave is a national monument.

The end of Mzilikazi's kingdom. Lobengula's Imbezu and Ingubu regiments are mown down by the Maxim guns of the British South Africa Company at the battle of Bembesi, 1st November, 1893.

The Ndebele Army

Like the Ndebele state itself, Mzilikazi's army was basically organized along Zulu lines, adapted to take account of the kingdom's peculiar circumstances and composition. From a nucleus of 300 Khumalo warriors, Mzilikazi steadily expanded his army, first by incorporating other Nguni refugees, then by absorbing both Sotho and, later, Shona subjects. The Ndebele population was never as large as its Zulu counterpart – the traveller Andrew Smith commented in 1835 that 'if [Mzilikazi] were called upon to muster every man he has in his country, he could not produce 4,000', and the total population in the Transvaal days was probably not more than 20,000. Even at its height in Matabeleland in the 1890s, after years of stable growth, it probably numbered no more than 100,000. As a result, Ndebele armies tended to be small, and most of the early battles were fought with forces numbering hundreds rather

Warrior of the Insuga, Lob-engula's young élite regiment. Note how similar the uniform is to that of the Imbizo.

than thousands. Some estimates of the Ndebele strength at Vechtkop in 1836 put it as high as 4,000 warriors – an interesting comparison with Smith's estimates – and there is no doubt this was an exceptional force, composed of almost every man Mzilikazi could muster.

Like his Zulu equivalent, the Ndebele king controlled his state man-power through the *amabutho*, the system of age-based regiments. Every few years he would call together all the youths who had reached the appropriate age and form them into a regiment. They would remain under his direct command until he gave them permission to marry and disperse several years later. In the Zulu state, this apparatus was an important means of unifying and controlling the various internal components of the kingdom. So it must have been amongst the Ndebele, though it was complicated by the fact that the various castes within the kingdom were not mixed together. Unfortunately, we simply do not have sufficient evidence to decide how this apparent contradiction was resolved. Certainly, during the early days in the Transvaal, some of Mzilikazi's Sotho vassal chiefdoms, which had not been fully integrated politically and culturally, supplied contingents of their own warriors for his army, and these were presumably armed and dressed in Sotho fashion. Later, amabutho were formed on a class basis, so that the army consisted of various regiments who were primarily Zansi, Enhla and, later, Holi in composition. The different groups were not mixed to-

Sketch by Harris of an Ndebele warrior. In the 1830s, the Ndebele retained much of their 'Zulu' appearance, including not only the characteristic weapons, but also the distinctive necklace of cows' tails.

Group of senior Ndebele chiefs, including Mtshane Khumalo (fourth from right), Lobengula's senior general, negotiating with Company officials at the end of the 1896 Rebellion.

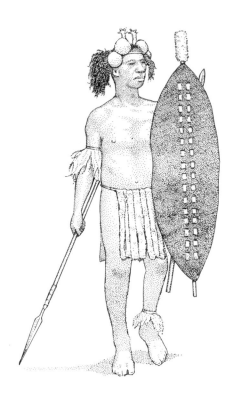

Young Ndebele warrior, or ijaha, *based on sketches made during Mzilikazi's stay in the Transvaal. By this time, some regiments apparently had adopted this unique headress, which consisted of inflated animal bladders, upright tubes of stiff hide, split at the tips, and black ostrich feathers.*

gether, because the Zansi, or pure Nguni, were considered the best fighting material, while the Holi were not highly rated. Presumably Nguni amabutho were kept up to strength initially by incorporating new arrivals of the same culture into their ranks. By the 1890s, many regiments had taken on a hereditary nature, as young men were drafted into their father's amabutho. This kept their class composition pure, but was clearly a significant break with the age-regiment principle.

Presumably, the amabutho were initially quartered in barracks, the equivalent of the Zulu *amakhanda*, throughout the kingdom. This certainly seems to be the case during the days in the Transvaal, where a number of large settlements were noted which were centres of royal authority. Later, in Matabeleland, there is a curious absence of references to such barracks, though the amabutho were still distributed throughout the kingdom. The king seems to have kept new regiments in direct service and under his personal control for no more than a few years, before he allocated them a particular district. At this point they seem to have married, and settled the area in personal homesteads. In this manner the king was able to control the internal colonization of his kingdom.

Most military service, particularly in Mzilikazi's reign, fell to the young, unmarried warriors, the *amajaha*. They formed Mzilikazi's strike force, and undertook most of the raiding, as they were considered physically more suited to it. The married men, the *amadoda*, formed a

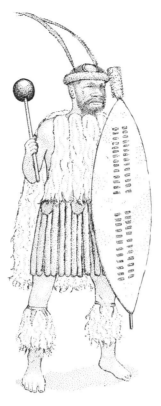

reserve, and were called out only in times of dire national emergency. During the wars against the Griqua, it was noted that the amajaha were daylight fighters, while the amadoda, being weaker, more often attacked at night. This no doubt reflects a pragmatic approach on Mzilikazi's part, for military manpower was a resource to be husbanded, not squandered in unnecessarily costly open attacks. Against enemies armed with spears the Ndebele employed the 'chest and horns' encircling movement usually credited to Shaka; indeed, it remained their standard manoeuvre as late as the 1896 Rebellion. Again, like the Zulus, the amadoda were distinguished by a ring of fibre woven into their hair, and plastered with black wax. The Ndebele ring seems to have been smaller, and worn further forward on the head, than was the custom amongst the Zulu.

The internal organization of the Ndebele amabutho seems to have been the same as for the Zulu, i.e. two wings subdivided into companies and commanded by izinduna appointed by the king. In Mzilikazi's time, each regiment was probably between 200 and 400 strong, and during the 1890s they averaged 600 warriors apiece. The traveller and artist Thomas Baines has left us a description of an Ndebele force returning from a raid in the 1860s, which suggests that they had lost none of the Zulu military discipline and flair. The warriors came

running in, two abreast, like troops coming on at the double. They turned off in succession to the right and then, facing toward the king, formed a close line, two deep, the shield of each man

137

overlapping that of the man on his right, and the successive regiments as they came in and joined the line, forming rather more than a semi-circle, dressed with a precision that would have charmed a military eye. . . . The commander-in-chief first came forward and narrated in order the progress of the expedition. They had gone in the direction they were sent, turning out to the right of their course and sweeping the country as they went, killing 186 persons, of whom 84 were women, and capturing very close on 3,000 cattle . . . the petty chiefs were allowed to come forward and boast of their deeds and then the various men who had distinguished themselves sprang out in turn running, leaping, crouching behind their shields, charging, retreating and stabbing in the air, gave one decisive stroke for each victim they had slain. . . .

Like their Zulu counterparts, each Ndebele ibutho had its own distinctive uniform. They carried oval shields of the Zulu pattern, and the colour on the face of the shield was part of the uniform, junior regiments carrying black shields and senior ones white. During the Transvaal, as Moffat's descriptions show, the Ndebele retained a very Zulu-like appearance. Ornate kilts of twisted furs were common, and cow tails were worn around the arms and legs. The basis of the headdress remained the Zulu headband, and senior men were similarly distinguished by crane feathers. However, as the Ndebele migrated, so they entered areas with different wildlife, and many of the old pelts and feathers of their Zululand days became unavailable. Gradually their military dress took on a style all of its own. In the Transvaal, headdresses were made of feathers from birds not found in Zululand and in Matabeleland, even during Mzilikazi's reign, Ndebele military costume became dominated by black ostrich feathers. In the 1860s, Baines shows amajaha wearing Zulu-style headbands, but with distinctive black plumes, and a shoulder cape of black ostrich feathers. By the 1890s the cape was universal and the headband had all but been abandoned. Instead, the headdress consisted of a large pon-pon of black feathers over the forehead, and a circlet of the same material around it. Generally, there is a noticeable decline in the quality of costume as the Ndebele move away from their Nguni origins, although the dress of the Zansi elite remained quite splendid.

Weapons were the Nguni throwing and stabbing spears. These, too, declined in quality, perhaps because the Khumalo fled Zululand without any expert smiths, and the Ndebele were never able fully to rectify this deficiency. Certainly, most Ndebele spears were less well made than the Zulu models. A number of non-Nguni weapons, including Shona spears and axes, were also widely carried. The Ndebele did acquire some guns from their fights against the Griqua, but the Griqua's own poor showing led Mzilikazi to be dismissive of their worth. In any case, supplies of powder and spare parts were nonexistent. During the later years of the kingdom large numbers of more modern weapons were obtained, but the Ndebele never fully integrated them into their tactical thinking and their potential was wasted. In 1893 they were still

Ndebele warrior in war-dress, 1893. In the field, the more precious or delicate items of dress were not worn, although a large pon-pon of ostrich feathers was generally retained. This man is armed with a Martini-Henry rifle. Rhodes had given Lobengula a thousand of such rifles to secure a prospecting concession before the war.

Dramatic sketch of an Ndebele charge, published at the time of the war with the British South African Company in 1893. The costume details are not inaccurate, but contemporary British engravings, naturally, represented the Ndebele at their most ferocious. Such images helped to justify Rhodes unwarranted intervention in King Lobengula's country.

Ndebele ijaha *(young warrior) photographed in the 1890s. His weapons and dress are fine examples of styles popular in the later period – although he is wearing the black ostritch feather headdress in an unusual fashion.*

mounting headlong charges against a European enemy armed with Maxim guns, with appalling consequences.

Mzilikazi's achievements were remarkable in many ways, but his skill in adapting an alien military system to suit his circumstances must rank high amongst them. The Ndebele army overcame a potentially crippling handicap, its cosmopolitan nature, to become a strong, united force which consistently bested a wide variety of African enemies. That it finally succumbed to a foe armed with a vastly superior technology reflects no shame upon it.

Bibliography

Bhebe, N. 'Mzilikazi' in Saunders, C. (ed) *Black Leaders in Southern African History*, 1979.

Harris, W.C. *The Wild Sports of Southern Africa*, 1839.

Moffat, R. *The Matabele Journals of Robert Moffat 1829–1860*, edited by J.P.R. Wallis, 1945.

Mziki (A.A. Cambell) *'Mlimo: The Rise and Fall of the Matabele*, 1926.

Omer-Cooper, J.D. *The Zulu Aftermath*, 1966.

Ransford, O. *Bulawayo: Historic Battleground of Rhodesia*, 1968.

Rasmussen, R.K. *Mzilikazi of the Ndebele*, 1977.

Rasmussen, R.K. *Migrant Kingdom: Mzilikazi's Ndebele in South Africa*, 1978.

Summers, R. and Pagden, C.W. *The Warriors*, 1970.

Chronology

1790s	Mzilikazi born. (Early white travellers gave various estimates of the exact year, choosing several dates between 1793 and 1799.)
1817	Mzilikazi installed as chief of the Khumalo.
1819	Mzilikazi offers allegiance to Shaka.
1821	Mzilikazi flees from Shaka and crosses into interior.
1822	Mzilikazi's followers attack the Pedi.
1823–27	The Ndebele settle in the southern Transvaal.
1825	The Griqua harass outlying Ndebele cattle posts.
1827–32	The Ndebele move north of the Magaliesburg mountains.
1828	JULY Jan Bloem's first attack on the Ndebele.
1829	OCTOBER First missionary visits to Mzilikazi.
1831	JULY Barend Barends attacks Ndebele.
1832	JULY First Zulu attack on Ndebele settlements.
1832–37	Ndebele move west and settle in Marico basin.
1834	MAY Jan Bloem's second attack on Ndebele.
1836	15 AUGUST Ndebele fall on Voortrekker hunting parties.
1836	15 OCTOBER Battle of Vechtkop.
1837	17 JANUARY Boer attack on Ndebele settlements at Mosega.
1837	JUNE Second Zulu attack.
1837	4–13 NOVEMBER Boer attacks on Gabeni; Ndebele abandon Transvaal.
1838–39	Ndebele migrate and establish new kingdom north of the Limpopo.
1847	Hendrik Potgieter discovers Mzilikazi's new location; threat of renewed Boer/Ndebele conflict.
1854	JULY Moffat visits Mzilikazi for the first time in years; start of renewed white contacts with Ndebele kingdom.
1868	5 SEPTEMBER Mzilikazi dies.

Maqoma

OF THE XHOSA

The earliest photograph of Maqoma, presumably taken during the 1850s, and showing him with his wives.

Three Xhosa chiefs, as they appeared in a rather charming engraving in the British press in 1864. All three are wearing the typical costume of men of rank: cloaks lined with leopardskin and crane-feather head-dresses.

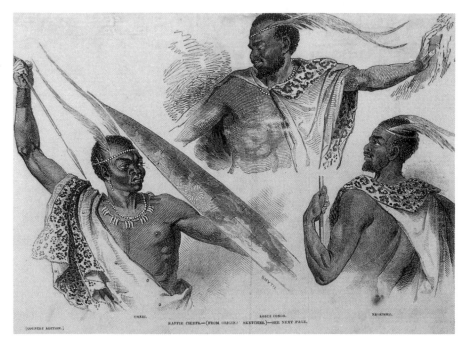

The Eastern Cape Frontier, showing the advance of the Colonial boundary from 1770 to 1847.

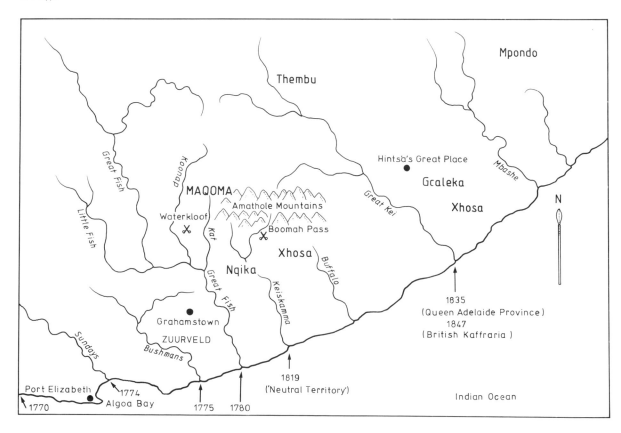

This is to teach you that I have come hither to teach Xhosa and that I am chief and master here, and in this way will I treat enemies of the Queen.

(Major-General Smith, his boot upon the subjugated Maqoma's neck)

You are a dog [a commoner] and so you behave like a dog. This thing is not sent by Victoria, who knows that I am of royal blood like herself.

(Maqoma's defiant response to Smith)

Proud and Tragic

Chief Maqoma of the Xhosa is in many ways a tragic, disappointed figure. He never became, as Shaka and other African leaders did, the architect of a new nation and, as the second-ranking chief of the amaNgqika section of the Xhosa people, he could never claim the pre-eminence he longed for and for which his talents so richly suited him. But he was the outstanding leader in the conflict between the Xhosa and white settlers, a fearless, daring and resolute warrior, undoubtedly the most able Xhosa commander to emerge from the entire century-long series of nine Cape Frontier Wars. The British, never slow to romanticize a dashing enemy, regarded him as something of a noble savage – 'a gallant bold fellow, and as a friend, a most excellent one; but as an enemy a very dangerous one', one officer wrote. Physically, he hardly fitted that mould, since he was below average height, thickset and powerful. He was not handsome, and had a broad face with a strong forehead from which his hair receded at an early age, and piercing eyes which revealed his strength of character. He was a clear thinker, a passionate orator and a dynamic man of action. A fervent nationalist, Maqoma was deeply proud, and clung to Xhosa culture. While he could be friendly towards individual whites, he saw nothing in them that was inherently superior, and he bitterly resented their racist contempt for black people.

There is no happy ending to Chief Maqoma's story. He witnessed the deliberate and systematic breaking of the Xhosa, and the reduction of his people to the level of a subclass within the expanding Colonial economy. For a while Maqoma himself seemed broken, and sought comfort in drink. When the wars were lost, he committed himself wholeheartedly to the Xhosa Cattle-killing movement, the last tragic gesture of a defeated people. As a result, the British humiliated him, sent him into exile, took his subjects away from him and impoverished him. Yet even as an old man he remained defiant, and refused to accept their authority. He died imprisoned on the notorious Robben Island.

The Angry Men

The Khoi, the original inhabitants of the Cape, called them the Chobona, after their greeting 'Sakubona (I see you)', or the Xhosa, 'the Angry Men', and it was this latter term the people themselves adopted. Classified by their language and culture as a branch of the southern Nguni, they have much in common with their famous northern cousins, the Zulus. Like the Zulus, they were a pastoral people who cultivated crops, but relied on cattle, not only for staple foods and clothing, but as a means of assessing wealth and status – cattle thereby governed all social relations. They were a polygamous people, each man marrying as many wives as he could afford to support, though in fact few commoners had more than one. Like the Zulus, they lived in family units, small clusters of thatch and daub huts arranged around a central cattle enclosure. They were grouped into clans, a rather vague and ill-defined social unit acknowledging mutual kinship, but their political structures were less rigid than those of the northern Nguni. Each clan had its own chief, but there was no equivalent of the *amabutho* system, whereby chiefs were able to organize and control clan manpower, which was to play such a pivotal role in the northern *mfecane*. A Xhosa chief's direct authority was limited to his councillors, and any young men serving him in the hope of winning bride-wealth. Beyond that, his powers were confined to his judicial and ritual functions. Much, therefore, depended on personal attributes – a chief who was just, wise, brave and, above all, generous, might attract and retain a large following, but one who was weak, stupid and mean would have very little influence because Xhosa commoners were free to attach themselves to new chiefs if they despised their own.

Sometime in the seventeenth century, a chief named Tshawe subdued the Xhosa clans, and from that time on his descendants dominated the Xhosa. Each of his male descendants was considered a prince of the blood, and each had the right to found a new chiefdom – 'You cannot have two bulls in one kraal', ran a local proverb. No one not of the amaTshawe ('Tshawe's people') could claim the rank of chief, and they regarded themselves as men apart. It was customary to refer to them by praise names such as 'elephant' or 'bull', while they called commoners 'black people' or 'dogs'. As chiefs they possessed certain hereditary privileges and commoners had to observe strict codes of etiquette in their presence. Nevertheless, ordinary Xhosa were greatly attached to their chiefs, who were seen as an embodiment of a common nationhood. Chiefs seldom killed one another, even in war, and it was a terrible crime for a commoner to do so – as Europeans would later discover to their cost.

The Xhosa trace descent from father to son. In a polygamous society, therefore, it was necessary to establish a hierarchy among the wives, and

the Xhosa divided them into the Great House and the Right-hand House. The Right-hand House was subordinate, and the heir to the chieftaincy was therefore the eldest son of the Great House. Tshawe's heirs were regarded as the senior family in the land, and their head was considered the paramount king of the Xhosa. The king's powers and responsibilities were only those of a chief writ large, however. He was responsible for presiding over the ceremonies which invested chiefs, for judging legal cases between junior chiefs, and for organizing national festivals, such as the annual first-fruits ceremony. His office was held in great respect, but he nonetheless lacked the power to interfere too closely in the affairs of his juniors. Important decisions had to be made in consultation with the chiefs, since no decision was binding on a subordinate chief who had not been present when it was made. Xhosa society acknowledged the right of both commoners and chiefs to ignore the king's rulings if he had proved himself unfit for the job. In fact, much of the king's power arose from the web of patronage and kinship obligations which flowed from his redistribution of wealth through judicial cases.

Since every son of each chief had the right to found his own chiefdom, Xhosa society was geared to permanent expansion. In the early days, when land was plentiful and the people few, this was not a problem. They drifted slowly down the southeastern coast of Africa,

Xhosa chief in traditional costume, based on a sketch by a British officer dated 1812. The shield was made of cowhide, but was less ornate than its Zulu counterpart; and was gradually abandoned once it had proved ineffective against European firearms. Most Xhosa fought naked apart from their cloaks: personal charms or provisions were often carried in a bag made of animal-skin and worn from a waist-belt of beads.

cut off from the interior by the barrier of the Drakensberg mountains, and following the pattern of good grazing pasture. They knew of the existence of the whites, because European sailors were occasionally washed up on their beaches, survivors of shipwrecks. One of our earliest descriptions of the Xhosa dates from 1636, from one such mariner: 'the men of the country are very lean and upright, tall of stature, and handsome.' As the coast stretched in a lazy curve westwards towards the Cape, a series of great rivers cut across their path, the Kei, the Buffalo, the Keiskamma, the Great Fish and the Bushmans. The bulk of the nation remained east of the Kei, but several more adventurous clans pushed on, entering the outlying districts settled by the Khoi people. Many Khoi were displaced, but others were absorbed, and the western Xhosa adopted many aspects of Khoi culture into their own. Then, about the beginning of the eighteenth century, the vanguard of the Xhosa first encountered white settlers, moving in the opposite direction. The stage was set for the grand struggle for land that would dominate the history of thc Xhosa. Yet, even as conflict loomed, fate decreed that the Xhosa would be unable to face the challenge with a united front, for the House of Tshawe was split in two by a fierce succession dispute.

The Dutch

The Portuguese explorer Dias discovered the Cape of Good Hope in 1488, but it was not until 1652 that the Dutch arrived to establish a permanent base there. It was already occupied by the Khoi – whom the Dutch called Hottentots – and by roving bands of San (bushmen) hunters. The Dutch purchased the Cape for a few trinkets and bullied the Khoi into submission. They built a mud fort, and planted vegetable gardens to provision the Dutch East India Company ships on the long haul to the lucrative Indies. Despite official disapproval, the small band of settlers gradually expanded, pushing their cattle-grazing, farming and hunting activities beyond the confines of the company's possessions, and by 1700 there were 615 free burghers – or Boers, as they were called – living at the Cape. They were a tough, independent-minded people, resentful of authority, whose restless spirit drove them into the wilderness in search of pastures new. The arid deserts of the Karoo, which lie north of the Cape, blocked them in that direction, so they turned eastwards, trickling down towards the hinterland of Algoa Bay. They were pursued by the Dutch authorities, who, resentful of the expense of establishing an administrative infrastructure, constantly tried to limit them by appointing new boundaries. The succession of rivers

Ordinary Xhosa warrior in traditional dress. In action, the cloak was wrapped round the left arm to protect the body, and the warrior carried spare spears in his left hand, throwing them with his right.

that lay before their path was ideally suited to the purpose. In 1770, the Gamtoos River was fixed as the Colonial border; but in reality it was already out of date, as there were Boer parties living well beyond it. A few years later, the boundary was pushed forward again, this time to the Zondaghs (or Sundays) River. By that time, the Boers had known of the existence of the Xhosa for more than half a century. Having difficulty in pronouncing that name, the Boers simply called them Kaffirs, a general term for black people which then lacked the offensive connotations it has since acquired. There were some early skirmishes, but for the most part both black and white found it profitable to trade, the Boers exchanging beads, copper and iron for cattle, ivory and skins. Inevitably, the Boers pushed forward across the Sundays, and into an area known as the Zuurveld, or Sour Veld, after the grasses which grew there, which made it good cattle country. But much of the Zuurveld was already occupied by the Xhosa, albeit thinly, and the patterns of settlement began to overlap. Some Xhosa groups had even penetrated far beyond the Sundays, wandering deep into Colonial territory. Since both groups required the same pasture for their cattle, the situation was potentially explosive.

In 1778, the Dutch governor visited the frontier and agreed a boundary with the local Xhosa. Unfortunately, he failed to realize that this agreement was not considered binding on any but those who signed it, nor did he address certain anomalies in the boundary itself. Tension continued to mount, the Boers complaining bitterly that the Xhosa refused to respect the border, were roaming throughout the territory as if they owned it and were stealing their cattle. The last accusation was probably just; young Xhosa did sometimes try to enrich themselves at some careless Colonist's expense. But cattle rustling was as much a symptom of discontent as a cause, for the Xhosa also resented the restrictions imposed by the Colonial presence. At this delicate moment, there was a sudden surge of Xhosa into the Colony. It was the result of a serious internal conflict, and it set the scene for a century of friction between black and white on the frontier.

Sons of Phalo

Maqoma was born in 1798, twenty years after the first treaty between the Xhosa and the Dutch, and his world was already shaped by a complex history of strife. He was the first son born to Chief Ngqika's Right-hand House, by his wife Notonta. As such, he was in the unenviable position of being the eldest son, but not his father's heir, a position reserved to offspring of the Great House. Not much is known about Maqoma's childhood, and no doubt it differed little from that of any Xhosa boy at the time. He would have grown up strong and athletic in an outdoor environment, and until puberty he would have been occupied herding his father's cattle. In due course he would have undertaken the various ceremonies attendant upon circumcision, which marked his transition to manhood. Circumcision ceremonies were held at the chief's discretion, whenever one of his sons was old enough, and included all those youths from his territory who had reached the appropriate age. While it lasted, the initiates were banished from normal society and lived in special temporary lodges where they underwent the ordeal. The ceremony fostered close bonds between those who experienced it together, and in later life circumcision-mates were expected to help and support one another. Because Maqoma was a chief's son, there would have been considerable prestige associated with sharing the ceremony with him, and many of those who did so would become his future councillors and personal followers. Once the ritual was complete, the lodges were burnt down, and the young men rejoined their families. It was only a matter of time before they struck out to establish their own homesteads, and no doubt Maqoma, whose military flair was apparent at an early age, would have considered clandestine cattle raids a suitable way to begin his fortunes. In this he would have had plenty of opportunities, since his childhood had taken

place against a background of turbulent times. Maqoma's father, Chief Ngqika, was an extremely important figure in these events, and his rise and fall were to shape Maqoma's destiny.

In order to understand something of his story, it is necessary to explore the rift within the House of Tshawe. It began with the reign of Maqoma's great-great-grandfather, King Phalo, whose reign was drawing to a close at about the time the Boers crossed the Sundays River.

Physically, Maqoma was scarcely the epitome of the European concept of 'noble savage'. He was broad, powerful, and ugly; yet his daring as a warrior earned him the reluctant respect of the British.

151

Phalo had a number of sons, two of whom were rivals for the succession. One was an aggressive and fearless warrior named Rharhabe; the other, the legitimate heir, was Gcaleka. Gcaleka was a sickly youth, who underwent a mystic experience known as *thwasa*, in which he experienced visions. In Xhosa society this marked him down as one touched by the spirits, and therefore qualified to be a diviner, with the power to identify and condemn those guilty of practising witchcraft. The implications for his brothers were disturbing – as Rharhabe commented, 'It is alright if ordinary black people *thwasa* – they are afraid to smell out [find guilty of witchcraft] a chief. But now that a chief has *thwasa*'d, who will escape being smelled out?' Rharhabe reacted by attacking Gcaleka, but, despite his reputation as a warrior, was defeated. While Gcaleka and his followers remained east of the Kei River, Rharhabe crossed to the west and began to build up his power by attacking the Xhosa clans already living there. This effectively split the House of Tshawe down the middle, and created two distinct sections, the *amaRharhabe* ('Rharhabe's people', often later called the *amaNgqika*) in the west, and the *amaGcaleka* in the east. Gcaleka's branch retained the kingship, while Rharhabe's branch bore the brunt of white expansion, and it is with them that we are primarily concerned.

Rharhabe's arrival west of the Kei caught those clans already living there between two fires, that of the aggressive newcomer and that of the Boers, who by now claimed the Great Fish River as their boundary. Rharhabe rampaged about, attacking Khoi and Xhosa alike. He did not long survive these wars, however, and died in battle in 1782. His heir, Mlawu, died with him, and control of his people passed to Rharhabe's son Ndlambe, who ruled as a regent for Mlawu's underage son, Ngqika. Ndlambe was a very able leader, a cunning politician and a warrior, and he was largely responsible for the rise of the amaRharhabe. In 1779 Ndlambe attacked the Xhosa imiDange clan, and drove them across the Fish River. The Boers complained to the governor, who authorized the use of force to drive them back again. Details of the fighting in this campaign, the First Cape Frontier War, are sketchy, but the Boers won one victory by tossing tobacco among a party of Xhosa. As the Xhosa scrambled to pick it up, the Boers opened fire, killing the Xhosa chiefs and most of their warriors.

In fact, apart from setting a ruthless precedent for future conflicts, this campaign did little to affect the situation on the frontier. Most Xhosa simply hid in the rugged hill country or bush-choked river valleys until the Boers dispersed, then returned to their homes. Its lessons were not lost on Ndlambe, however, who at once realized that the Boers were potentially a most useful ally, who could be manipulated to his own ends. In 1793, as part of his campaign to subdue the Xhosa west of the Kei, he proposed to the Boers that they mount a joint raid on those Xhosa still in the colony. The Boers delightedly agreed. This was the start of the Second Frontier War, which ended when the Boers drove Ndlambe's enemies out of their territory and straight into his army. Ndlambe won an easy victory.

With this triumph, Ndlambe secured ascendency over the amaRharhabe, but, even in the hour of his victory, a new threat rose against him. His ward, young Ngqika, the legal heir, suddenly rebelled. According to tradition, Ngqika's councillors whispered in his ear, 'You see, Chief, the *Maduna* [Big-Shot] is running away with your people, for they have become accustomed to him. Go, pretend you are paying a courtesy visit, and we shall attack him'. Taken by surprise, Ndlambe fled, complaining loudly of his nephew's ingratitude. His friends the Boers failed to support him, so Ndlambe appealed to the Xhosa king. For all their old rivalry, the House of Gcaleka recognized the justice of Ndlambe's appeal, and sent a force to his aid. Ngqika intercepted it; in an epic victory, he defeated it and took Ndlambe prisoner.

Ngqika was scarcely eighteen, and he had burst upon his people like a young Apollo. According to the description of one traveller who visited him, he was handsome, charismatic and intelligent; 'the name of [Ngqika] was in every mouth, and it was seldom pronounced without symptoms of joy.'

It was no accident that that particular commentator was British. In 1795 Britain had displaced the Dutch as rulers at the Cape, in one of the side effects of the Revolutionary Wars in Europe, and the mission to Ngqika was part of a fact-finding tour to establish their policy on the frontier. Ngqika, like Ndlambe before him, simply regarded them as a new factor to be used in his own political struggles. At the height of his power, he saw no reason to fear them, and he was most certainly not in awe of a white skin, sharing the view of most Xhosa that '[they] never think the white men are more wise or skillful than themselves, for they suppose that they could do all that the white men do if they chose'. The British envoys suggested to Ngqika that the frontier question would be simplified if those clans living west of the Fish were to retire east of it, and Ngqika, smiling, agreed. He would later learn to his cost the terrible price of his alliance so easily entered into.

In any case, the British were to be disappointed with this simple solution. When they suggested to the Zuurveld chiefs that they retire into Ngqika's territory and throw themselves on amaRharhabe mercy, they received an indignant refusal. Clinging to the policy of enforcing the border of the Fish, the British moved troops to the frontier, and the Third Frontier War (1799–1802) broke out. It was no more conclusive than its predecessors, though it did give the British a taste of what was to come; fighting the Xhosa, the British commander reflected, was 'an unequal contest with savages in the midst of impenetrable thickets' which would add 'little lustre to British arms'. Few of his successors would disagree with him.

Chief Ngqika, Maqoma's father, and a bright star amongst the western Xhosa at the beginning of the nineteenth century. Ngqika's misguided alliance with the British led to his decline.

The Fall of Ngqika

In 1800, Ngqika must have felt every satisfaction with his position. He had made new allies in the British, who were even then attacking his rivals across the Fish, and his rival Ndlambe was lodged safely at his Great Place. Small wonder that he took to calling himself *inkosi inkulu*, 'the Great Chief', or even 'king of the Xhosa', both titles reserved for the paramount. Such was his success that he had indeed eclipsed the House of Gcaleka across the Kei. But, even at the moment of his triumph, events turned against him.

In 1800, Ndlambe escaped from Ngqika's custody, and fled across the Fish and into the Colony. Here he took advantage of the war then raging to gradually rebuild his position. Ngqika appealed to his allies to return him, but in 1803 there was another change in the regime at the Cape. Patching up a dubious peace on the frontier, the British sailed away, to be replaced by the Dutch, this time under the banner of the Batavian Republic. The new governor toured the scene of conflict, and met Ngqika at an impressive conference in which the chief complained bitterly of the injustices he had suffered from his uncle. The governor was sympathetic, but the truth was that the Batavians' lacked the resources to mount a campaign to drive Ndlambe out of their territory. Indeed, their reign was a brief one, for in 1806 the British once more occupied the Cape, this time permanently.

Ngqika's frustration was intense. In 1807, he resorted to the stratagem of kidnapping one of Ndlambe's wives, a renowned beauty. Presumably he intended to provoke Ndlambe to come out of hiding and attack him, but his plan misfired disastrously. In taking his uncle's wife, Ngqika had committed, in Xhosa eyes, a particularly dreadful form of incest. His scandalized followers began to desert him, and overnight his prestige evaporated. Ndlambe did indeed attack him, and Ngqika was defeated, and forced to flee to a mountain retreat, where he began to drown his sorrows in European liquor.

The British, meanwhile, began to exert their authority. They accepted their predecessors' view that the Great Fish boundary was not negotiable and, after careful consideration, decided that the Xhosa living east of it must be removed. Most of these had, by now, given Ndlambe their allegiance. Ndlambe refused to move, however, and in December 1811 the British took the bull by the horns and decided to force him out. Troops were moved to the frontier, and, with a ruthless efficiency lacking in previous Frontier Wars, drove them across the border. Ndlambe, still defiant, fled the Colony and into Ngqika's territory. The British sealed the frontier with a chain of blockhouses and established a new administrative centre in the border region which they called Grahamstown.

Despite his defeat, Ndlambe's prestige was boosted by his stand against the British, and he had no problem in rebuilding his power. In this he was aided by a prophet named Nxele, a mystic who claimed to have the ability to turn white men's bullets to water. Ndlambe and his followers continued to raid cattle across the Colonial border, and in 1817 the governor, Lord Charles Somerset, well aware of the divisions between the Xhosa, met Ngqika to offer him support in return for his help against cattle rustling. Ngqika agreed, despite the fact that he was in no position to enforce such an agreement.

Here, at last, we have our first glimpse of Maqoma, standing beside his father at the conference with Somerset. He was not long out of the circumcision lodge, and perhaps had already taken part in the incessant skirmishing with Ndlambe's people. Certainly his strong personality was already earning him followers, and when the struggle between Ngqika and Ndlambe came to a head, Maqoma was selected to lead his father's armies. Ndlambe moved rapidly to try to crush the threat posed by his rival's treaty with the British, and in October 1818 Maqoma led the amaNgqika into the foothills of the Amathole mountains to intercept him. The armies met on an undulating plain known to the Xhosa as Amalinde, after the saucer-shaped depressions which scar its surface.

The battle of Amalinde was perhaps the last epic contest of Xhosa tradition. Maqoma led the vanguard of younger warriors, known as the *ingqukuva*, or 'buds', into the thick of the fight, and Ndlambe's warriors broke under the onslaught. As the amaNgqika chased them from the field, however, Ndlambe's reserve, which had been hidden in a nearby forest, suddenly charged down and caught them in the flank. Maqoma and his bodyguard, most of them his circumcision-mates, tried desperately to rally their forces, but it was too late, and the Ngqika scattered. Maqoma stubbornly refused to leave the field until at last he was badly wounded and his companions carried him away. Ndlambe's jubilant warriors hunted down their enemy until dusk, and then lit great bonfires so that they could see in the darkness to finish off the wounded.

In desperation, Ngqika appealed to the British, claiming that Ndlambe had attacked him because he was opposed to cattle rustling in the Colony. The British responded by sending a punitive expedition which rounded up some of Ndlambe's cattle. When it retired, Ndlambe's angry warriors swept into the Colony, and the Fifth Frontier War began. Its climax came in April 1819 when Nxele in person led an audacious attack on Grahamstown itself. In one of the few pitched battles of the wars, the Xhosa attacked in massive columns, and the British drew up to receive them in parade-ground formations. Sadly, Nxele's promise that the bullets would turn to water proved false, and his followers paid dearly for their faith. Over a hundred warriors were cut down by British muskets and artillery fire, and as many as a thousand were wounded. The victorious British swept into Ndlambe's territory, destroying everything in their path. The war ended only when Nxele himself surrendered.

Xhosa headress of the type worn by young men not long out of the initiation lodge. It consists of two bunches of blue-grey wing feathers, stitched into a buff skin headband.

Ngqika was exultant at his rival's misfortune. He and Maqoma were often to be seen in the British camp, where they

amused the young officers by showing their dexterity in poising the spear before putting it deep in an ox, which Ngqika pierced through on one occasion, at such exhibitions laughing all the time, with Maqoma, at the white man's credulity. Whenever the officers presented wine or brandy to Ngqika or Maqoma they invariably made Ngqika's bushman servant, Plaatje, taste it before they drank.

But not all of Ngqika's followers were happy with his alliance with the British. A Boer companion, a renegade who had fled the advent of British rule and established himself at Ngqika's court, had warned him not to trust them. Using a metaphor for ruthlessness which the Xhosa well understood, he had described them as 'the bushmen of the sea'. When the British presented Ngqika with the bill for their help, Ngqika found out what he had meant.

South Africa was one of the few fields of war where the British army gradually adopted practical styles of campaign dress. As early as 1835, forage caps were being worn in the field instead of the heavy shako; and locally made trousers and cartridge belts were worn in preference to the hot, heavy and impractical regulation issue items. This is a private of the 72nd Highlanders.

Bushmen of the Sea

Governor Somerset had a comprehensive new plan to resolve the frontier conflict, and at a meeting with Ngqika in 1819 he blandly informed him that the British would be extending their territory east to the Keiskamma River. The new slice of land that they had therefore acquired, known, somewhat euphemistically, as the 'ceded territory', would be a neutral zone. Neither whites nor blacks would be permitted to live there, though a line of military posts would be erected to prevent Xhosa incursions. The Xhosa had just one month to evacuate their settlements. In vain did Ngqika protest that this territory was his traditional land, the place of his birth. He was in no position to argue, and his followers had little choice but to do as they were told, though the lasting effect of Somerset's policy was to alienate the amaNgqika. Ruefully, Ngqika complained 'that though indebted to the English for his existence as a chief, yet when he looked upon the fine country taken from him, he could not but think his benefactors oppressive'. Inevitably, cattle rustling increased.

The neutral territory was one aspect of a broader Colonial plan devised by Somerset, which also included increased European settlement on the frontier, and an insidious attempt to westernize the Xhosa and undermine their economic and cultural independence. In 1820, large numbers of British settlers, easily recruited during the economic depressions which had followed the Napoleonic Wars, were brought to South Africa and unceremoniously dumped along the border. In many cases the land granted to them was inadequate to support them, and few had any idea of the skills they would need to survive in the bush. Many did not last the course, but, after several years of hardship, the frontier district began to take on a distinctly British flavour, with small hamlets springing up bearing names such as Bathurst and Woburn. In addition, missionaries were officially encouraged to preach amongst the Xhosa, and, after a shaky start, regular trade was established across the neutral territory.

The 1820s marked the emergence of Maqoma as a chief in his own right. His father Ngqika's decline was accelerating. What little power Ngqika had depended on white support. He used his links with the British to bully his rivals with threats of military action, and he had no qualms about blaming others for thefts committed by his own followers. He regularly attended the trade fairs organized at Fort Willshire, where he shamelessly begged for presents. He was often seen drinking in military canteens, and he became addicted to European liquor. Small wonder that, in 1822, Maqoma judged the moment right to leave his father's Great Place and establish a chiefdom of his own.

With typical daring, he chose an area of the Kat River. This was within the neutral zone, but the Colonial authorities were prepared to allow him to stay providing he behaved himself. The area was already settled by a band of Khoi, whom Maqoma absorbed into his following. He then began to build up his herds, and the basis of every chief's material wealth, by raiding the Thembu people, who were the Xhosa's northeastern neighbours. The Colonial authorities watched this with concern, but when they appealed to Ngqika, they received a surprising reply. Ngqika was jealous of his son's growing prestige, and simply advised the Colony to 'go at once to [Maqoma], without waiting to see whether he returns the Tambookie cattle and attack him, fire upon him and his people, and take his cattle, and then after that to reason with him.' On several occasions they followed his advice, though Maqoma simply tendered his apologies and carried on much as before.

The 1820s also witnessed another threat to frontier stability. The continuing violence in Natal to the north had squashed some of the clans there down into the territory of the amaMpondo, the Xhosa's northern neighbour, and a handful of refugees had even reached Gcaleka territory. They were to form the nucleus of a people known as the Mfengu, from the verb *ukumfenguza*, 'to wander about seeking service', and their ranks were swollen by Xhosas impoverished by the British campaigns and by mission converts, who did not fit easily into Xhosa society. They were given shelter in return for service, and they contributed to some extent to the re-emergence of Gcaleka power under the capable King Hintsa.

The old rivalry between Ndlambe and Ngqika was drawing to a close. In February 1828 Ndlambe died, a fierce old warrior still respected by his people, and the power of the amaNdlambe was frittered away in a succession dispute between his sons. In 1829 Ngqika himself

Hintsa, Chief of the Gcaleka Xhosa, and paramount King of the nation. Hintsa was betrayed and murdered by Sir Harry Smith, a crime which left a deep impression on the Xhosa people.

died of a combination of drink and tuberculosis. His power and prestige had long since gone, and only his looks remained to testify to the glory of his youth – and to what might have been.

Ngqika's heir was his son by his Great Wife Suthu, a boy of eight or nine years old named Sandile. Clearly he was too young to rule, and he had four adult brothers, Anta, Xhoxho, Tyhali and Maqoma. The amaNgqika chose as their regent Maqoma, and there can be no doubt that he was ideally suited to the role. Within a very short space of time, therefore, with the collapse of the amaNdlambe and the death of Ngqika, Maqoma had suddenly emerged as the most significant of the western Xhosa chiefs.

Unfortunately, he had also become an implacable enemy of the Colony.

Maqoma's War

In 1829, Maqoma had raided the Thembu again, and the Governor's patience gave out. Troops were sent into the Kat River valley, and Maqoma and his people were driven out of their settlements and their huts destroyed. As far as Maqoma was concerned, his attacks on the Thembu were a purely local affair and were no business of the Colonial authorities. He therefore regarded his expulsion as a great injustice and it poisoned his relationship with the Colony forever. For a while, the commandant on the frontier, recognizing the very real hardship Maqoma was suffering, let him graze his cattle on his old lands, but, in 1833, he was expelled again. Maqoma believed the British were deliberately making a fool of him. His lands on the Kat were given to Khoi thought loyal to the Colony, but many of Maqoma's own followers were Khoi, and there was much sympathy between them. In October 1833, a missionary at the settlement held a tea party, and invited Maqoma to attend. This was illegal under the terms of his expulsion, but he went anyway. Maqoma took the opportunity to make a speech which suggests something of his bitter frame of mind at the time:

I see no Englishmen in the Kat River, there are none in Grahamstown, and where are they? I have got them all in [Xhosaland], with their wives and children, living in safety and enjoying every protection: and yet I am accounted a rascal and a vagabond, and am obliged to come here by stealth.

Someone at the party objected – 'for making religion a cloak for inducing this savage to disobey laws and regulations intended for the safety of the community' – and the troops were summoned. A sergeant and six troopers of the Cape Mounted Rifles rode up. The attitude of the sergeant was variously described as friendly or drunk, and he offered the chief a bottle in front of his hosts. Bitterly humiliated, Maqoma was hustled away, and out of the settlement. When Maqoma had been expelled the second time, the officer went to enforce the order commented:

He distinctly said, which we found out afterwards to be the case, that he could not make out the cause of his removal, and asked me if I could tell him; and really I could not; I had heard nothing; no cause was ever assigned to me for the removal.

Maqoma's reaction was predictable, he was 'very violent; the man was very much irritated', and his subsequent mistreatment at the tea party only inflamed his anger and sense of injustice. According to Chief Bhotomane, '[Maqoma's] heart was very sore about the land; the subject always set him on fire; he fought in hopes of getting it back'. Maqoma was convinced that the British action was part of a wider plan to dispossess the Xhosa, and told his fellow chiefs that the British behaviour was the 'prelude to other measures, which would not only endanger their independence, but lead to a complete subjugation of their country'. The chiefs were inclined to agree. As his brother Tyhali said, '[Ngqika] was a great friend of the white people. And they murder his children after he is dead.'

In this tense atmosphere, an unfortunate incident convinced the Xhosa that the English did literally intend to murder Ngqika's sons. In December 1834 Maqoma's brother Xhoxho was defiantly herding cattle in the neutral territory. He was accosted by a British patrol, and in the ensuing scuffle, a shot was fired which grazed his head. The Xhosa were thunderstruck. A chief's life was sacrosanct, and by wounding one in the head, the British had quite clearly been prepared to kill him. The reaction was universal and spontaneous:

every [Xhosa] who saw [Xhoxho's] wound went back to his hut, took his [assegai], and shield, and set out to fight, and said 'It is better that we die than be treated thus . . . Life is no use to us if they shoot our Chiefs.'

On Monday 22nd December 1834 the Xhosa rose up and rushed into the Colony.

This, the Sixth Cape Frontier War, was very much Maqoma's war. He and Tyhali decided upon a strategy, which, as was the custom with a major undertaking of this importance, they submitted to King Hintsa for approval. The Gcaleka east of the Kei had so far stood aloof from conflict with the whites, but Hintsa considered the treatment meted out to the chiefs and gave his consent to war. Maqoma and Tyhali had very definite objectives. They intended to strike at the centres of settler authority and force the Governor to the negotiating table. Maqoma's first objective was to take the trading post of Fort Willshire. There were many Khoi within the post who were sympathetic to the Xhosa, and Maqoma counted on them to open the gates and allow his warriors to enter. In the event, they failed to do so, and Maqoma's attack on the

A private of the Cape Mounted Rifles, a British Imperial unit raised locally for use on the Frontier. The CMR wore dark green jackets and caps and buff leather trousers. They were armed with swords and double-barrelled percussion carbine, which was a particularly effective weapon in bush-fighting. Although all the officers were white, a high proportion of the other ranks were Khoi.

bastions failed. Instead, he took his warriors across the Kei, and fell on the exposed farms and villages of the settlers. The Xhosa rampaged through the Colony, killing, burning farms and driving off livestock. A Boer settler has left a vivid impression of a night attack on his farm:

> The [Xhosa] whistle and shout on all sides; shot, assegais and stones fall on the house almost like rain. The sheep bleat, the cattle bellow, the dogs bark, the enemy rush in and cut the cattle loose, others attempt to storm the house, one [Xhosa] is shot dead in the doorway with a stabbing assegai in his hand. The commotion was fearful.

The frontier garrisons hastily retreated to their forts, and for a while it looked as if Grahamstown itself might fall. But the Xhosa attack gradually spent itself, and the tide turned in January when Colonel Harry Smith, an energetic veteran of the Peninsular Campaign, arrived to take command. Smith galvanized and bullied the local inhabitants – he had a brief meeting with the commandant of the frontier, Henry Somerset, and ever afterwards dismissed him as 'an ass' – and, ignoring the bands roving the Colony, he went on the offensive. The Xhosa retired before him to their traditional strongholds, the Fish River bush and the Amathole mountains.

The Amatholes feature strongly in the Xhosa struggle, and particularly in Maqoma's part in it. Physically, they are a circle of hills rising up from the headwaters of the Keiskamma and Buffalo rivers, a maze of interconnecting ridges and deep, bush-choked valleys. It was difficult country for a European army:

> It is in fact one of nature's labyrinths. Its sides are bold and precipitous; it is split and intersected by ravines; it is broken by masses of rocks, and it is clothed with noble forest trees . . . altitude is considerable and they are thickly belted, and in some parts covered with thick bush. Masses of craggy rock here and there rise perpendicularly amidst these thickets, and in other parts the sides of the mountain are deeply scored by kloofs, or rocky gullies covered by rank vegetation.

It was to this wild country that Maqoma and Tyhali retired, waging a skillful guerrilla war. Gone were the mass attacks of the pre-Colonial age. Instead the Xhosa ambushed wagon trains as they laboured through the bush. Patrols were lured into rough country by decoys of cattle, then cut off and massacred. The case of Lieutenant Charles Baillie and thirty men was typical. Baillie set off on a sweep through the Amathole, and agreed a rendezvous next day with another detachment. His party failed to show up. The other party waited as long as they dared, then returned to base. For several weeks it was hoped that Baillie's party was on some secret mission – lying in wait to capture Maqoma, was a favourite theory – but his party was never seen again. After the war, a warrior told how they had been decoyed into the bush and surrounded in a river bed; 'We closed upon them, and destroyed them all. They fell in one heap; and in a ravine you will find their bones'.

Exasperated by such warfare, Smith decided on a new strategy. Convinced of Hintsa's complicity in the Xhosa attack, and with Governor

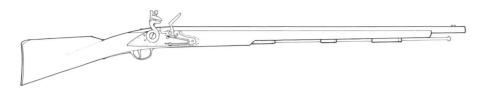

D'Urban's support, Smith struck across the Kei. The Gcaleka were not officially at war with the Colony, and as his troops forded the Kei, a Xhosa called out 'Hello, English! Do you know what river this is?'. But Smith was not to be deflected, and he rampaged through the countryside, raiding and burning. In an attempt to stop him, Hintsa accepted Smith's guarantees of safe conduct and entered his camp. The British agreed to call off their incursion into Gcaleka territory providing Hintsa agreed to tell the Ngqika chiefs to lay down their arms and to pay a large indemnity in cattle. While the negotiations were going on, Hintsa was prevented from leaving Smith's camp. Then a new factor was added to the negotiations.

According to the traditional view, the Mfengu had become dissatisfied with life under the Gcaleka umbrella – they explained their treatment by saying that the Xhosa had offered them food, but that it had been placed on the Xhosa side of the fire, and the Mfengu had to pass their hands through the flames to reach it. Smith claimed that they appealed to the British for sanctuary. Their request was granted, and the Mfengu collected up their possessions and prepared to march into the Colony with the British, much to the disgust of the Xhosa. A more recent critical analysis suggests that many of these Mfengu were in fact Xhosa, whom Smith had captured during his invasion and whom the British now kidnapped to fulfil the labour demands of the frontier, where they were settled as a buffer against Xhosa incursions. Economically dependent on the whites, they would fight against the Xhosa in future campaigns, and relations between the two were permanently soured. Whatever the truth of the Mfengu exodus, Smith then set out to round up the required Gcaleka cattle, taking Hintsa with him as a hostage for good conduct. Seizing his chance one day, the paramount king of the Xhosa tried to escape, and Smith ordered his men to open fire. Hintsa, wounded through the leg and body, took refuge beneath the banks of a stream, where a young volunteer found him and blew his brains out. After his death, someone in Smith's force cut off Hintsa's ears and kept them as a souvenir. Smith thought his death was no more than he deserved, but the legacy of this brief expedition would bear a bitter fruit. The Gcaleka would never again trust the British, and when news of the murder reached Maqoma and the other Ngqika chiefs, they decided to fight on. A desultory skirmishing continued for month after month in the Amatholes.

In the end, peace came not because the chiefs were defeated, but

A 'Brown Bess' flint-lock musket, typical of thousands which entered Xhosaland from the middle of the nineteenth century. Once the Napoleonic Wars ended, obsolete firearms were dumped on unsophisticated markets around the world. This example has suffered badly from termites attacking the wooden stock, a fate which undoubtedly befell many others.

because both sides were tired of war. D'Urban was becoming seriously alarmed at the expense of the war and the criticism in Britain of Hintsa's death and he was keen to bring the fighting to a close. Using mission converts as go-betweens, he offered the chiefs terms. Throughout August and September a series of meetings took place which Maqoma and Tyhali attended personally. They, too, wanted an end to the fighting, but did not consider themselves defeated; on one occasion they listened patiently to the British offer, politely thanked the men who delivered it, then rejected it and went back to war. At last, however, D'Urban agreed to meet some of their grievances, and on 11 September they entered Fort Willshire and laid down their arms.

Imperial Retreat

Maqoma and Tyhali had won political concessions as a result of their continued defiance. D'Urban had originally intended to expel all Xhosa west of the Kei, but he had to abandon this plan to secure peace. The amaNgqika would be allowed to retain their lands – even the Amathole – but they would be incorporated within the Colony. The area between the old ceded territory and the Kei was added to British possessions and given the name Queen Adelaide's Province. The chiefs would become British subjects, and the man chosen to administer them was none other than Colonel Harry Smith.

Smith was, to say the least, an eccentric character. Restless, flamboyant, supremely egocentric, he threw himself into his new task with a will. Fondly imagining that he understood the Xhosa and their ways, he took to calling himself *inkosi inkulu*, 'the Great Chief', and referring to the Xhosa as his 'children'. He organized elaborate meetings intended to overawe them with British might, holding court with a variety of theatrical props, his favourite being a brass-headed cane which he wielded as a staff of office. He forced respected Xhosa chiefs to prostrate themselves at his feet, and made effusive and melodramatic speeches. He distributed especially designed medals and gaudy uniforms to his favourites, whom he would publicly embrace with tears in his eyes. His plan was to bring the Xhosa gradually within the Colonial administrative system, and he built a series of military posts across the Province and introduced British magistrates to oversee the chiefs. The chiefs accepted his bizarre behaviour with patience, but they were not fooled. Behind his back, Maqoma 'often turned to ridicule the fine speeches that were delivered, and the imposing scenes which were displayed', but he knew, too, how to flatter. Smith, who had considered Maqoma 'a remorseless and relentless savage', was surprised at his subtle mind, and admitted that he 'knew more theology than many Christians'. Maqoma's charm won him more land.

Yet Smith's rule was destined to be short. The British government was appalled when it received the details of Hintsa's death, and, after an enquiry, decided that 'the [Xhosa] had ample justification of the war into which they rushed'. It refused to ratify D'Urban's agreement. Queen Adelaide's Province was to be abandoned, and Smith recalled.

To replace him, a Colonial official named Andries Stockenstrom was appointed Lieutenant-governor, with the responsibility of implementing a new frontier policy. He abandoned Smith's military posts and magistracies and instead adopted the 'treaty system', the underlying principle of which was that all dealings with the chiefs should be conducted on an equal footing, recognizing their independent status. The chiefs, relieved to be free of Smith's indignities, were pleasantly surprised by this even-handed approach, and years later Maqoma would declare 'I will hold by Stockenstrom's word until I die and my people put me in my grave. If the treaties are forced from us, nothing can preserve us from war.'

Yet the treaty system did have bitter enemies. D'Urban, still in office, gave it no more than nominal support, and it was hated by the settler community. As far as they were concerned, they had done nothing to warrant their sufferings in the recent war. The Xhosa had been justly punished for their aggression, and it had been right to appropriate their land. They saw the retrocession of Queen Adelaide's Province as an imperial retreat, and they resented Stockenstrom's attitude towards the 'few thousands of ruthless worthless savages [who] sit like a nightmare upon a land that would support millions of civilised men'. The survival of Stockenstrom's system was clearly questionable in any case, but his position was further undermined by a prolonged drought which again swept through the area in the 1840s. The Xhosa sought relief in cattle rustling, to the settlers' noisy disgust. Stockenstrom relied on the chiefs to prevent it – 'I am a policeman', grumbled Maqoma, 'I fall on the spoor [trail] daily' – but the social dislocation caused by years of war had produced a class of bandits who lived beyond the control of the chiefs. In 1840 Stockenstrom bowed to the inevitable and accepted early retirement.

Maqoma, meanwhile, had worries of his own. In 1842 his brother Sandile came of age and was presented to Stockenstrom's successor as the rightful heir of the amaNgqika. Sandile was quiet and thoughtful, but he had a withered leg, and he lacked Maqoma's powerful presence, so his personal prestige was low. Maqoma despised him as an idiot, and was driven to fury by the knowledge he would have to give up his regency and the power that went with it. In 1842 he spotted an opportunity to retain his position. His former ally Tyhali was dying of tuberculosis, and Maqoma accused Sandile's mother, Suthu, of bewitching

Chief Sandile, painted by Frederick I'Ons in the 1850s. Maqoma was forced to give up the regency of the amaNgqika when the rightful heir, Sandile, came of age. Maqoma was bitterly resentful of the man he considered an idiot: yet Sandile, whilst certainly not as decisive as his brother, would still emerge as a champion of Xhosa independence. He was killed in action in the Ninth Frontier War.

Maqoma as sketched by Angas in the 1840s, when his fortunes were at their lowest ebb. Frustrated and impoverished, he took refuge in alcohol, but returned to wreak vengeance on Harry Smith in the Eighth War.

him. If proved, such a charge would have irrevocably tainted Sandile. Tyhali recognized his purpose – 'Maqoma wishes, when I am dead, to eat up my people, and destroy [Ngqika's] house'. In the event, the Colonial authorities got wind of the plot, and intervened. Suthu was saved, but the effect on Maqoma was disastrous.

A man of fierce passions, he was eating himself away with frustration. He ached for his Kat River lands, he resented the treatment dished out by the whites and he hated Sandile. He had a liking for strong liquor, and he began to spend more and more time at the military canteen at Fort Beaufort. Private Buck Adams of the 7th Dragoon Guards saw him often, 'about 45 years of age, clad in a very large and handsome kaross, a coil of common large beads around his neck, and on his feet a pair of patent leather Wellington boots, with large red tassels hanging down in front of them.' Adams, more sympathetic than most of his colleagues, noted the ferocious quantities of wine and 'Cape Smoke' (strong peach brandy) downed by the chief and his entourage. 'I believe there had been times when the whole of them had been drunk long before sunset', he commented sadly. '[Maqoma], the Chief, was always the first to get drunk, and the rest very soon followed suit.' The Colonial authorities, believing alcohol would keep Maqoma quiet, cynically allowed him a weekly ration of a gallon of brandy. At its height, his drinking impaired his ability to rule as a chief – Tyhali claimed 'when my messengers went to him he was always drunk, and knew not what he said'. A British official concluded 'He is now more or less deranged in his mind. Several medical men have declared him insane. He certainly is so occasionally . . . I believe his only desire is to get strong drink.' When drunk, Maqoma was liable to fly into uncontrollable rages, and was said to mistreat his family. Yet it is easy to overemphasize his alcoholism, for, while he certainly sought escape through drink, he would later prove himself more than capable of shrugging off his addiction.

While Maqoma regularly drank himself into a stupor, the Xhosa and the Colonists slid into another war. The British had lost faith in the treaty system, and a succession of governors adopted a harder line with the Xhosa. Matters came to a head in March 1846 when a Xhosa was arrested for stealing an axe from a trader. He was arrested, but on his way to jail his friends attacked the escort and rescued him. In the ensuing skirmish one man was killed. The Colonial authorities were convinced that this was a calculated act of defiance by young Sandile, and demanded that the murderers be handed over. Sandile was unable to comply, and a column was despatched to attack his settlement at Burnshill in the Amatholes. The force was accompanied by a large wagon train, and as it wound slowly through a particularly thick stretch of bush, the Xhosa suddenly attacked on all sides. The troops were unable to form up properly, and the Xhosa easily overran the centre wagons, driving off the oxen and escaping with guns, ammunition and the regimental silver of the 7th Dragoons.

The ensuing War of the Axe followed a familiar pattern. After the

Colonial troops search a deserted camp in the Perie Bush in the Ninth Frontier War. A dead warrior, wounded in previous fighting, can be seen on the left. The scene is reminiscent of the final sweeps through the Waterkloof in September 1852.

victory at Burnshill, the Xhosa poured into the Colony and besieged the settlements. Gradually the troops mustered against them, and drove them back to their strongholds. This was the first war in which the Xhosa made extensive use of firearms and horses, both gained in illicit trading with the merchants of Grahamstown. It made them an elusive and dangerous foe, but they were still no match for British regulars in the open, as the battle of Gwangqa in June proved. Here a British cavalry column stumbled across a Xhosa army moving across its front, and in the ensuing charge scattered them to the four winds, inflicting dreadful casualties. Such battles were rare, however, and both sides resorted to a war of attrition, the British destroying Xhosa settlements and crops, the Xhosa burning farms and attacking supply trains. In the end, the British army proved the better able to withstand these tactics and the Xhosa chiefs were starved into submission. In October, Sandile agreed to visit Grahamstown to discuss peace and, like Hintsa before him, was promptly arrested. The war fizzled out by the end of the year.

Maqoma had played little part in the fighting, sulkily refusing to join Sandile's war. In June he had accepted the government's assurances of good treatment and been moved to live under supervision at Port Elizabeth.

Inevitably, the end of the War of the Axe saw a new settlement imposed on the Xhosa, and, to Maqoma's surprise, it brought the return of a familiar face to the frontier. It was sufficient to jolt the chief into sobriety.

War of the Riverman

In December 1847 a new governor arrived at the Cape, none other than Harry Smith, now knighted and promoted to Major-General as a result of his recent victories in India. His ego had blossomed beyond all control. He spoke openly of himself as 'the Hero of Aliwal', and he organized a triumphal procession from the Cape to the frontier. Bands played, crowds cheered, and the recently defeated Xhosa chiefs were required to pay public homage. As he landed at Port Elizabeth, Smith noticed Maqoma in the crowd. He stared deliberately at the Chief, then drew his sword half from its scabbard, before dropping it back 'with an expressive gesture of anger and scorn'. The startled chief stepped back, and the crowd laughed delightedly. Later that same day, Smith sent for Maqoma in his hotel, and, again before an audience, made the chief kneel. Smith placed his boot on Maqoma's neck. 'This is to teach you', he cried 'that I have come hither to teach [Xhosaland] that I am chief and master here and in this way shall I treat the enemies of the Queen.'

It was a bitter and unnecessary insult. Maqoma's response is remembered as, 'You are a dog [a commoner] and so you behave like a dog. This thing was not sent by Victoria who knows that I am of royal blood like herself.' It was the beginning of a deadly personal feud, and in time Maqoma would have his revenge.

On the frontier, Smith organized more of his theatrical meetings with the Xhosa chiefs. Under the eyes of his massed troops, Smith set up two poles with ornate heads which he called the 'Staff of Peace' and the 'Staff of War'. Each chief was required to choose and touch one or the other. Tearing a sheet of paper into shreds, Smith threw it melodramatically into the air, shouting 'No more treaties!' On one occasion he blew up a wagonload of gunpowder to demonstrate what would happen if the Xhosa 'dared to make war' again. The chiefs, subdued by their recent hardships, accepted all this meekly. Chief Bhotomane, asked what he thought of Smith's manner, replied drily 'The day was stormy – the wind blew very strong.'

Chief Myango, the son of Sandile, in a splendid study, probably taken early in the twentieth century. Although his dress consists of nothing more than a blanket and a head cloth, his rank is suggested by the richness of his personal ornaments – his beads and ivory bracelets.

The basis of Smith's policy was that the old ceded territory was to be opened for white settlement, while the land between the Keiskamma and the Kei was to be annexed to the Crown as British Kaffraria. It was Queen Adelaide's Province by any other name. Military posts were to be established throughout the region, and the chiefs' conduct was to be supervised by resident magistrates. Various Xhosa practices that Smith disapproved of were outlawed, including the exchange of bride-wealth – the basis of all marriage customs – and the 'smelling out' of witches.

It was a familiar package for the Xhosa. The ban on smelling-out ceremonies particularly disturbed them, as in their eyes it allowed evil-doers free reign. Once again, the country was suffering from drought, and the nation was afflicted by misfortune. Such a climate was ripe to produce a religious leader, another Nxele, and sure enough one emerged in the form of a sickly young man named Mlanjeni. Mlanjeni was touched by the spirits at an early age, and spent much of his time sitting in pools of the Keiskamma River purifying his body and soul – for this reason he was known as 'the riverman'. Mlanjeni claimed that the nation had been polluted, but that by sacrificing certain types of cattle it could regain the level of purity necessary to drive out the troublesome whites once and for all. Like Nxele, he distributed charms and promised invulnerability from the white man's gunfire.

The chiefs were disturbed by his message, though it spread like wildfire among ordinary Xhosa. Sandile, the head of the amaNgqika, was cautious, wary of embarking on another war so soon, but Maqoma, throwing off the mantle of the broken alcoholic, burning with resentment at his treatment by Smith, was resolute. 'I want the whole country to know that Maqoma is not mad', he said, 'for at the time of the Axe War they said I was mad.'

Smith steadfastly refused to recognize the signs of discontent. He was once more esconced in his role as the inkosi inkulu, and he was convinced that his Xhosa 'children' would gradually come to see the benefits of civilization he was bringing them. He made another tour of the frontier, and tried to bully the chiefs once more. 'Tell them', he blustered, 'that in four days I can have my ships at the Buffalo River with thousands of soldiers.'

'Yes', snapped back Maqoma, 'but have you got any ships that will sail into the Amatholes?'

Smith dismissed Maqoma as 'a drunken beast', and decided on a show of force. He despatched a column into the Amathole foothills. On 24 December 1850 it entered a bushy defile known as the Boomah Pass. Once it was well inside – 'a pack oxen stuck in the mud', as the Xhosa idiom had it – the Xhosa attacked. The column was barely able to extricate itself. The next day the Xhosa swept into the colony.

The resulting conflict, the Eighth Frontier War, was the longest, most comprehensive and most destructive of them all. Almost all the

By the time of the Eighth Frontier War in the 1850s, most British soldiers fought in undress shell jackets, with a variety of locally acquired civilian hats and trousers. The harsh life of campaigning in impenetrable thickets in all weathers also took its toll. As a result, the uniforms soon bore little resemblance to parade-ground dress.

168

Ngqika chiefs joined it and Hintsa's successor, Sahrili, gave his tacit support. Many Khoi, disenchanted with the mistreatment they had received at colonial hands, also rose up, and the Thembu in the north-east, hitherto uninvolved in any conflicts with whites, fought to regain a slice of the territory Smith had arbitrarily taken from them. Smith, temporarily trapped in one of his forts, was beside himself at the ingratitude and 'treachery' of the Xhosa. Unable to mount any effective military response, he watched helplessly as the Xhosa rampaged through the Colony, destroying many of the new settlements.

Nevertheless, the Xhosa were as unable as ever to storm fortified posts, and after a month away from their homelands they had trouble provisioning themselves. The attack was spent, and Smith regrouped and went on to the offensive. He vented most of his spleen on the unfortunate Khoi – 'we destroyed [their] fort by fire, a great many men, women and children were destroyed by fire in the fort', wrote a participant in one incident – and drove the Xhosa back into their main retreats, the Amatholes and the Fish River bush. Both would require long and brutal campaigns of suppression.

From the beginning, Maqoma had been one of the leading Xhosa generals. At first he operated in the Amatholes with Sandile, but in April 1851 he slipped into the Kroomie mountains with a Khoi leader, Hans Brander. The Kroomie were a western spur of the Amathole, and were part of Maqoma's old lands in the Kat valley, for which he had yearned so long. They were split by a series of interconnecting rugged valleys, which the British knew as the Waterkloof. This was to be Maqoma's stronghold – or Den, as his enemies called it – throughout the war, the base for his far-ranging and highly successful raids and the heart of his defences. On 7 September 1851 Colonel Fordyce of the 74th Regiment took his men into the Kroomie mountains in the first attempt to drive Maqoma out. After a long climb in the heat, they reached the peak of a ridge overlooking the Waterkloof. Fordyce's plan

Sketch by Thomas Baines called 'A War Dance in the Amatoles'. It captures the dramatic beauty of the Xhosa stronghold. By the 1850s, many Ngqika Xhosa had adopted items of European clothing.

was to descend into it and comb the bush, but first he allowed his troops to fall out for lunch. No sooner had the men unbuckled their equipment than there was a tremendous shout, and the Xhosa suddenly poured out of one of the gullies and attacked. Fordyce's men formed up to repel the charge. One of them saw a Xhosa in European clothing – Maqoma himself – ride into the open and dismount, issuing commands to his men, though attracting a good deal of British fire. He was directing them to cut off the route by which Fordyce had ascended, but the movement was spotted and intercepted. The Xhosa broke off the attack and Fordyce decided his position was too exposed and began to retreat. On the steep, wooded path Maqoma struck again, his warriors 'yelling in the most diabolical manner, hissing through their white teeth: their faces bloody, brawny limbs, and enormous size, giving them a formidable appearance.' The column finally emerged at the bottom of the slope in complete confusion leaving thirteen dead behind and carrying a number of wounded.

This first action set the pattern for the Waterkloof campaign. Maqoma's forces were probably small, but their command of the terrain was masterly, and they ran rings around the clumsy British forays:

Day after day officers and men tore their way through the thick jungle without seeing an enemy and yet as we approached or left a kloof the shots fired at us showed us they were there. Colonel Fordyce of the 74th Highlanders . . . was positive that the place was deserted. He had come

Highlanders versus the Xhosa: the 74th Regiment attacking a Xhosa position.

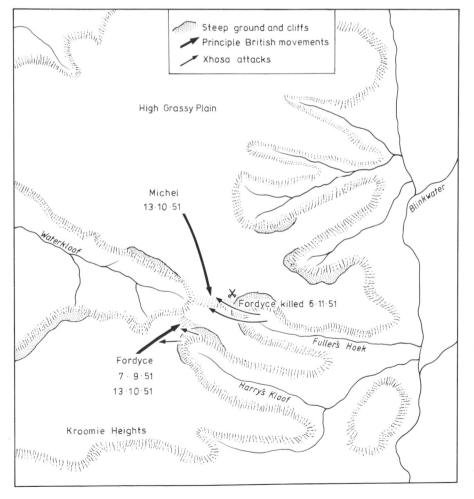

The early fighting at the Waterkloof, site of Moqoma's great battles of the Eighth Frontier War. The British tried repeatedly to seize a high ridge which linked Kroomie Heights to the plateau above and which commanded both Fuller's Hoek and the Waterkloof. However, they were repulsed by the Xhosa emerging from the dense bush and steep crags of Fuller's Hoek.

The strategic key to the Waterkloof was a narrow ridge leading from the Kroomie Heights up to a plateau beyond, and commanding the valleys of the Waterkloof on one side, and Fuller's Hoek on the other. Here, the 74th Highlanders are shown as they fire down from the ridge into Fuller's Hoek.

through it with his whole regiment in skirmishing order without firing a shot. The next day he was killed.

Fordyce was killed on 4 November, standing to issue orders during a firefight. As he fell the Xhosa yelled exultantly 'Johnny bring stretcher! Johnny, bring stretcher!' There could be no doubt who was winning the struggle. As a local newspaper commented, 'Maqoma remains proud master of the field. He has outgeneralled the First Division. He has cut down its men, and for the remainder he must entertain something very nearly approaching to supreme contempt.'

Smith, growing increasingly desperate, fell back on his old strategy of striking across the Kei. In two raids he drove the Gcaleka before him and returned with an enormous herd of looted cattle. This did something to boost morale in the Colony, and he was able to marshal his forces for a fresh attack on the Waterkloof. Maqoma's Den was bombarded, his personal huts destroyed and a number of women from his household captured, but the chief himself and most of his fighting men escaped. It was not enough to save Smith's reputation. In March 1852 he received a stiff note from the home government criticizing his policies and terminating his command.

It might fairly be said that Maqoma had had his revenge.

The fighting had, in any case, already entered a new phase. Smith had set the tone earlier when, in a fit of pique, he called on the settlers

Scene showing Xhosa warriors
returning from a successful cattle raid with a herd looted from
Colonial farms.

'to destroy and exterminate these most barbarous and treacherous savages.' As the war progressed, the British became increasingly ruthless,
and their tactics, masterminded by Lieutenant-Colonel Eyre, began to
bear fruit. Eyre, energetic and forceful, refused to be defeated by the
terrain, whipping his men forward with his riding crop, rolling pack
animals down slopes they refused to descend, and generally dragging
the war into areas hitherto considered impenetrable. His attitude towards the enemy was equally tough and his men shot, bayoneted and
cut the throats of warriors and civilians alike. The frustration of a long,
hard campaign was fast eroding whatever humanitarian feelings the
whites may have had towards the Xhosa. 'I could feel no compunc-
tion', one young officer wrote in a letter home, 'do you know, dear
Mother, in shooting a [Xhosa], and yet I could not shoot a dog without
feeling some pity . . .'. Xhosa crops were deliberately destroyed, huts
burned, men, women and children killed, their bodies left on public
display and their skulls taken as souvenirs. The final sweeps through the
Waterkloof read like some macabre medieval Triumph of Death:

We saw two [Xhosa] hanging in the trees, just been shot as the blood was trickling from the
forehead.

The place stunk horribly from the bodies of dead [Xhosa] that were lying about.

As we ascended the evidences of the fight became more frequent; rolling skulls, dislodged by
those in front, came bounding down between our legs; the bones lay thick among the loose

stones in the sluits and gulleys, and the bush on either side showed many a bleaching skeleton.

Not even Maqoma could stand in the face of such an onslaught, and he and his surviving followers slipped away to the Amatholes. Mercilessly harried, the formidable Xhosa army of 1850 was gradually reduced to a few guerrilla bands. By the beginning of 1853 they were starved, brutalized and exhausted, and they could not hold out much longer. On 2 March they agreed to meet the new Governor, Sir George Cathcart, and accepted his terms for surrender.

Waiting for the Dead Chiefs

The War of Mlanjeni had cost the Xhosa dearly, but Cathcart's peace was not as harsh as might have been expected. At first, he toyed with the idea of expelling the amaNgqika beyond the Kei, but decided that this would create as many problems as it solved. Instead, the Ngqika were banished forever from the Amatholes and squeezed into a cramped and impoverished reserve on the western bank of the Kei. Much of their former land was parcelled out to their enemies, the settlers and their Mfengu allies. The chiefs were allowed to maintain their authority, but a magistrate was appointed to oversee each of them.

The amaNgqika languished in their reserve. 'I cannot live with comfort on these flats where there is no bush', one said, '. . . my cattle are always turning their heads towards the [Amatholes]'. Then, in 1853, the cattle disease lung-sickness swept right across Xhosaland. The Xhosa had no cure for it and watched horror-struck as thousands of head of cattle sickened and died. The very heart of the nation seemed diseased, and the people ached for a cure that would return them to their former glories.

It is, perhaps, scarcely surprising that they sought one at the hands of a religious prophet. Nxele had promised salvation, but had proved false. So, too, had Mlanjeni, and for a while, as the warriors gained their first successes, it seemed as if he spoke the truth. But he too had lied, and, like thousands of his countrymen, he had not survived the war that bore his name. Now a new prophet arose, a young girl named Nongqawuse, who claimed to have seen visions one misty morning in April 1856, by the mouth of the Gxarha River in Gcalekaland. She had seen the horns of an immense ghostly herd of cattle below the waves, and Ndlambe, Ngqika, Hintsa and all the dead chiefs had appeared to her. They told her they were waiting to return to the land of the living and to sweep the white race from the face of the earth. In order to bring about this miracle, Nongqawuse urged the Xhosa to destroy their crops and kill their cattle.

Curious as it sounds, Nongqawuse's prophecy was consistent with Xhosa beliefs. Sacrifice was an essential part of their religious life, and it required no great leap of faith to see that an exceptional sacrifice was needed at a time of exceptional malaise. Furthermore, rumours of curious happenings began to circulate, which supported Nongqawuse's claims. Governor Cathcart left the Cape to fight in the Crimea, where he was killed leading his troops at the battle of Inkerman. The Xhosa had never heard of the Russians, and firmly believed they were really the army of long-dead warriors. Many ordinary Xhosa began to slaughter their herds, and when the king, Sahrili, visited Nongqawuse and announced his support for the movement, it spread like wildfire.

Across the Kei, the Ngqika wavered. Sandile was inclined to disbelieve, but Maqoma, clutching at a final straw to stave off the ruin of his people, threw his weight behind the movement and pressurised Sandile to do the same: 'are you a chief and led by black men [commoners]? . . . What other chief has been likewise led? Show your authority . . .'. Tension mounted between believers and unbelievers, then broke into open violence. Those who risked everything were not prepared to see their own hopes dashed because of the non-compliance of the faithless.

At first, the British watched the movement with alarm, fearing that it was a prelude to another uprising, but gradually the Colonial authorities, led by the Governor, Sir George Grey, came to see it as a solution to their own problems. Nongqawuse declared that the apocalypse would take place in February 1857. The sun would turn blood red, she claimed, darkness would cover the land, and the dead chiefs would arise. The believers ecstatically awaited their deliverance, but on the appointed days the sun rose and set as usual, and the people woke up to their predicament. They were starving.

For several months, Xhosaland was a scene of the most horrendous devastation. Whole homesteads simply starved to death, and bodies littered the wayside. Bands of destitute and hungry people walked to the nearest Colonial settlements to beg for food:

Many died by the way. One poor old man was found dead with his head hanging over his corn-pit. He had gone with his last breath to look if it had not yet been filled, and, falling, never rose again. Those who reached us were the most pitiable figures, breathing skeletons, with hollow eyes and parched lips. The innocent children looked like old men and women in miniature . . . Day after day, day after day, as these spectres came in crowds and crawled along, one might have imagined that the prophet's prediction had come to pass, and that the dead had indeed risen from their graves. . . .

Sir George Grey reacted to this crisis with all the charity of the Victorian workhouse. He offered no official assistance and discouraged acts of private compassion. He saw it as an opportunity to break the spirit of the Xhosa once and for all. He offered them contracts of employment with white employers. Those who accepted the harsh terms, which bound them for years and usually involved transportation from their homeland, could be saved; the rest must fend for themselves. It was an excellent opportunity to destroy the power of the chiefs, and Grey's magistrates harried them mercilessly. Maqoma was one of them. He had staked everything on the movement, and it had failed. He lashed out at nonbelievers around him, and again took refuge in the bottle. He was implicated in the murder of a police spy named Fusani. Grey wanted him convicted, but a court found no evidence against him. Nevertheless, Grey 'thinks that although [Maqoma] has been acquitted of the murder of Fusani, he is morally responsible for that murder, committed by persons acting under his orders'. Maqoma was sentenced to death, which Grey graciously commuted to twenty years imprisonment. Thus were the great warrior chiefs of old to be removed from the frontier, to make way for European civilization.

Maqoma and his colleagues were destined for imprisonment 'Esqithini', 'on the island' – the grim and desolate Robben Island off Cape Town, which was home to generations of South African political prisoners. They travelled there in chains. Maqoma's were 'heavy enough for a ship's cable', but he bore them proudly, and even at the end hoped for a chance to plead his case once more to Sir George Grey. But there was to be no such chance, and the Xhosa chiefs were shipped across the water, to serve out their sentences in a bleak settlement consisting of Xhosa huts, covered with tarpaulins instead of thatch. Their existence was spartan. They were allowed to keep goats and hunt hares, and some had their wives with them. Gradually, as it became clear that there was no hope of an early release, they sank into despair. Maqoma's wife Katyi fell sick and died rejecting medicine, wanting no more of life.

Maqoma was amongst the last to be released. In 1869 he was allowed back to the frontier, but found the Xhosa changed. Sandile and Sahrili were still nominally head of the Ngqika and Gcaleka, but their real power was gone, their followers scattered and broken, and their land claimed by whites. Maqoma clung to his defiance – 'old [Maqoma] is exhibiting a restless spirit and has been using contemptuous language to the authorities', complained a local settler. Clearly his yearning for his old home was undiminished. In August 1871 he was intercepted on the outskirts of Fort Beaufort with two wagons, twenty followers, and 150 head of cattle. He claimed he had bought land in the Waterkloof and was on his way to occupy it. The police turned him away. Two months later he tried again and was arrested at night in a hut near the Kroomie heights. He was taken straight to a steamer for Robben Island.

This time he was alone. On 9 September 1873, the great Xhosa general and nationalist died, aged 74. His last act was to complain bitterly of 'being here alone – no wife, or child, or attendant.' The authorities buried him without ceremony in a common unmarked grave.

A group of Xhosa chiefs
photographed on Robben
Island, where they were exiled
after the Cattle Killing tragedy. Maqoma is the bald man
sitting on the right. Life on the
Island was bleak and empty.

The Chiefs Siyolo (left) Maqoma and Xhexho, upon their
release from Robben Island in
1869. Maqoma's power as
broken, but his will to resist
was undiminished.

Four years later, the Xhosa rose up for one last time. A quarrel between a party of Mfengu and some Gcaleka flared into a faction-fight, and the colonial authorities were drawn in, protecting their Mfengu allies. Sahrili called out his warriors, and Sandile – asking 'how can I sit still when [Sahrili] fights?' – joined him. But the times were too far changed, and the Xhosa were broken by breach-loading rifle and artillery fire. Sandile took to the Amatholes, acting the part of the warrior chief of old. On 29 May 1878 he was killed in a firefight with the Mfengu. The rising collapsed.

There is a curious sequel to Maqoma's story. In 1978, Chief Lent Maqoma, his great-great-grandson, secured the permission of the South African authorities to allow a partially sighted, disabled albino seer, Miss Charity Sonandi, to visit Robben Island in an attempt to find Maqoma's grave. Miss Sonandi went straight to an unmarked plot and cried 'It is the Chief! Take him home!'. When the grave was opened, it

Sandile's son Matanzima, probably photographed around 1878 at the end of the Ninth War. He is wearing a luxurious cloak of leopardskin, and carrying a heavy spear for close-quarter fighting and a northern Nguni-style shield.

was found to contain remains consistent with those of Maqoma. The remains were placed in a coffin, carried on board a naval ship to Port Elizabeth, and there landed with a guard of honour. The body was taken to a spot near Ntaba kaNdoda, a prominent peak in the Amatholes, and laid to rest in the presence of 10,000 Xhosa on Sunday 13 August.

It is, of course, impossible to be certain that the remains were those of Maqoma, and there are those who remain skeptical about the whole incident. There can be no doubt, however, of the genuine desire of the Xhosa people to honour their greatest hero more than a century after his death. Whether in body or spirit, Chief Maqoma had, indeed, come home to rest.

Retreating Xhosa carry away their wounded on oxen after an unsuccessful attack on a colonial blockhouse.

The Xhosa Military System

The lack of a strong central government among the amaXhosa meant that there was little in the way of an organized army. There was no

179

The incompatability of Xhosa and British modes of warfare cut both ways. Captain Bambrick of the 7th Dragoon Guards, 'accustomed to charge wherever the foe might be' is surrounded and killed in the bush on 11th April 1846, at the start of the 'War of the Axe'.

equivalent of the amabutho system, which gave the northern Nguni chiefs so much control over their manpower, and a Xhosa chief could only command, at his own homestead, a handful of men who were economically dependent on him. The king could not compel his chiefs to join him in a war, nor could chiefs compel commoners, though it was unusual for them to refuse a summons. When a particular king or chief decided on war, it was usual for him to explain his reasons, since a good cause and clan loyalty were the factors that decided the extent of his support. Warriors rallied to leaders known for their daring and skill, such as Maqoma, or to chiefs who patronized a charismatic religious leader like Nxele or Mlanjeni.

When a chief decided on war, he made the formal declaration – '*Ilizwe ilfile*', 'the land is dead' – and sent his heralds, carrying leopardss' tails, to rally his followers. Women spread the news throughout his territory by passing on a distinctive shrill cry from hilltop to hilltop. The warriors wore no distinctive costume. Everyday male dress consisted of nothing more than a penis sheath, and perhaps some beads around the waist and arms, and a cloak of bullock-hide, worked to great suppleness and coloured with red ochre. Youths recently out of the circumcision lodge wore a headdress consisting of a band of hide

Xhosa war-dance depicted in a sketch, which although it was made during the Ninth – and last – Frontier War, still captures the traditional appearance of the Xhosa, with their hide cloaks and throwing spears.

around the forehead, with bunches of blue-grey wing feathers stitched to either side, and men of rank or distinction wore single crane feathers, distributed by the chiefs. Chiefs themselves wore cloaks lined with leopard-skin. Once at the chief's Great Place, the warriors underwent various ceremonies designed to render them invulnerable in the coming fight. This often included the distribution of magic charms – Mlanjeni, for example, gave his followers a twig from the plumbago bush to ward off evil.

On the march, a Xhosa army could move swiftly across rugged terrain which was impassable for a European army. There was no commissariat, beyond a few head of cattle driven with the army, and most warriors carried no more supplies than a few roasted corncobs in a hide bag. On campaign they were expert raiders and foragers, but this complete absence of a supply system probably explains why their sweeps into Colonial territory ground to a halt after a few weeks. Unlike the Zulus, whose military outlook was geared to offensive action, the Xhosa were equally at home defending their mountain or forest retreats.

In pre-Colonial times, battles were fought in the open, and tactics were similar to the more famous Zulu 'chest and horns' encircling movement. In the Xhosa equivalent, young warriors would take the centre, while more experienced men would form on either side the two 'wings' that would try to rush out and surround the enemy. A chief was expected to show daring without recklessly endangering himself, and he usually took up a place to the rear, along with his bodyguard, composed of his circumcision-mates and called *amafanenkosi*, 'those who die with the Chief'. The battle of Amalinde, in which Maqoma 'learned to tie and milk the kicking cow', or saw action for the first time, was the last of the great formal inter-clan battles. In fighting Europeans, the Xhosa soon learned that frontal attacks were suicidal, as this description of their helplessless before the British muskets of Grahamstown suggests:

While kneeling and ducking in front of the troops, the right hand was always raised with the assegai but their fear of looking at the fire prevented them from throwing as often or as correctly as they otherwise might have done. On seeing a flash they immediately placed the left arm with the kaross [bullock's hide] before their eyes.

Xhosa weapons consisted of a bundle of throwing spears, and perhaps a cow-hide shield. These were similar to the Zulu type, but less well-made, without the characteristic double rows of lacing. They could stop a flung spear, but they were no use against a musket ball, and their use died away as the Xhosa took more and more to fighting the Europeans in dense bush, where shields were impractical. In battle, a warrior

From the 1840s, the Xhosa began to use large numbers of firearms, though they were usually outdated flint-lock types. Those who had contact Iwith Europeans also began to wear items of cast-off clothing. This man is wearing a mixture of dress which became increasingly common in the wars of the 1850s and 1870s. He is also wearing a black head-cloth and a trade blanket.

would hold his spears in his left hand, and wrap his cloak around his arm, and rush down on his enemy throwing his spears with his right hand. As he did so he gave them a quivering motion which added to their accuracy in flight and imparted greater penetrating power. A skilled warrior could hit a target easily at ranges up to fifty yards. A flung spear had considerable velocity and could easily skewer its victim right through; it was by no means a weapon to be despised, and the accounts of British soldiers suggest that they hated it. Most fighting was conducted at spear-range, but sometimes the order 'Phakathi!', 'Get inside!', was given to signal a rush to hand-to-hand fighting. In such cases a heavier spear might be used for stabbing, or the hafts of throwing spears broken off to make them easier to use. In the early Frontier Wars, the Xhosa were sometimes successful in overwhelming European parties by closing in before they could reload, and fighting at such close quarters that the whites were unable to use their muskets.

The Xhosa were quick to understand both the limitations and advantages of guns. They took firearms from dead soldiers, and, later, an illegal trade in guns and powder flourished along the frontier. By the

Xhosa ambushing a British column in dense bush – a favourite tactic which was repeated time and again during the Sixth, Seventh and Eighth Wars. The Xhosa readily took to firearms, although obsolete weapons and poor ammunition greatly reduced their effectiveness.

A skirmish in the bush during the Sixth Frontier War. The Xhosa preferred to fight in the bush, where their opponents movements were severely hampered, and small parties could be cut off and over-run.

time of the War of the Axe the Xhosa were using firearms in such large numbers that it began to affect their tactics. However, their guns were usually of the poorest quality, and ammunition and spare parts were always in short supply. Nevertheless, the successful attacks on the wagon trains at Burnshill and Boomah Pass owed much to Xhosa firepower. They also acquired horses in large numbers, which added to their effectiveness as raiders.

Perhaps the most significant aspect of Xhosa warfare throughout the later Frontier Wars was their use of the terrain. Unable to compete with regular troops in the open, they were nonetheless masters of their own landscape. Unencumbered by supply trains and personal equipment, they could move through thick bush, following game trails that were invisible to whites. They were experts at concealment and ambush. A favourite tactic was to try to lure enemy parties away from their main body, by using individuals or cattle as decoys. In this they were often successful. On one occasion, a single Xhosa warrior stepped out of the bush, prompting a patrol to fire at him. Before they could reload, more Xhosa burst out from hiding and charged in among them. The fate of Lieutenant Baillie's party, drawn into the bush, then surrounded and massacred, was by no means unique. Parties of Xhosa would often

appear at a distance from a patrol, and shout out challenges and insults. This not only added an element of personal confrontation to a fight, it served to make the enemy break ranks and follow them. 'You are like a mouse in a calabash', a Colonial unit once heard a triumphant Xhosa shout, when they fell into such a trap, 'you have got into it, but you cannot get out!' The British became increasingly frustrated by such

Xhosa warrior photographed late in the nineteenth century with traditional throwing spear and knobkerry; and he wears a trade blanket in place of a hide cloak. His shield is northern Nguni, a style which spread south during the mfecane.

warfare, and, rather than confront it directly, turned increasingly to a war of attrition. It was easier to subdue the Xhosa by burning their homes and crops than it was by defeating them in battle.

Traditional Xhosa battles were seldom very destructive, and the life of a chief was held in great respect, even by his enemies. In the early Frontier wars, the Xhosa sometimes behaved magnanimously towards whites, sparing women and children, and even men known to have done them no harm. As time went on, however, the wars became increasingly ruthless. Europeans did not always differentiate between friendly and hostile Xhosa, nor even between warriors and women and children, provoking massacres in return. The Xhosa used to mutilate enemy dead, disembowelling them to free their spirits, and believing that parts of their bodies were a potent source of war medicine. This disgusted and horrified the whites, and may partly explain their own barbaric treatment of Xhosa dead. By the 1850s racial attitudes were such that few whites considered the Xhosa human beings. They were slaughtered indiscriminately and their skulls and bones were often collected as trophies. In return, the Xhosa had long since lost any compassion for their enemy. The grim scenes in the Waterkloof and elsewhere were the logical result.

Bibliography

King, W.R. *Campaigning in Kaffirland, or Scenes and Adventures in the Kaffir War of* 1851–2, 1853.

Milton, J. *The Edges of War: A History of Frontier War,* 1702–1878, 1983.

Pieres, J.B. 'Ngqika', in Saunders, C. (ed) *Black Leaders in Southern African History,* 1979.

Pieres, J.B. *The House of Phalo,* 1981.

Pieres, J.B. *The Dead Will Arise,* 1989.

Smith, Sir H. *The Autobiography of Sir Harry Smith,* 2 vols; 1903.

Soga, J.H. *The South-Eastern Bantu,* 1930.

Chronology

1652	First Dutch settlement established at Cape.
1778	First attempt to fix a boundary between the Cape and the Xhosa.
1779–81	First War on the Eastern Cape Frontier.
1793	Second Cape Frontier War.
1795	First British occupation of Cape.
1798	Maqoma born.
1799–1802	Third Cape Frontier War; the ascendancy of Ngqika.
1806	Second British occupation of Cape.
1811–12	Fourth Cape Frontier War.
1818	OCTOBER Maqoma's baptism of fire at the Battle of Amalinde.
1818–19	Fifth Cape Frontier War; Battle of Grahamstown.
1820	Influx of British settlers on Cape frontier.
1822	Maqoma establishes a homestead on the Kat River.
1829	Death of Ngqika; Maqoma becomes regent of amaNgqika and is expelled from Kat River district by the British.
1833	Maqoma humiliated at missionary tea party.
1834–35	Sixth Frontier War; murder of Hintsa.
1842	Sandile comes of age; Maqoma loses the regency, and enters decline.
1846–47	Seventh Frontier War 'the War of the Axe'.
1847	Return of Harry Smith to Cape frontier; he insults Maqoma.
1850–53	The Eighth Frontier War 'the War of Mlanjeni'. Maqoma's Waterkloof campaign.
1856	Start of the Cattle-killing movement.
1857–69	Maqoma exiled to Robben Island.
1871	OCTOBER Maqoma exiled again to Robben Island.
1873	9 SEPTEMBER Maqoma dies.

Index

Page numbers in *italics* refer to illustrations; text references may occur on the same page.

Illustrations

Photographs on the pages listed are reproduced, with thanks, courtesy of the following: Africana Library, City of Johannesberg – pages 20, 96,119, 135, 147 and 177; South African Library – pages 50, 57, 69, 81, 85, 157, 163 and 169; Cape Archives Depot, Department of National Education – pages 61, 111, 142, 151 and 153.

Other photographs are reproduced from the author's collection courtesy of the following: S.B. Bourquin – pages 18, 37 and 46; Natal Museum – page 17; Killie Campbell Library – pages 6, 11 and 178; McGregor Museum – pages 23, 91 and 167; Emil Wessells – page 35; Administrators Voortrekker Monument – page 121; National Archives of Zimbabwe – pages 115, 125, 139 and 140.

All other photographs are reproduced courtesy of the author's own collection.

Maps and line illustrations from the author's references were specially drawn for this book by Peter Komarnychyj.